More Praise for "The Naked Career"

"Brings a refreshing way to review career progress, for any employer, employee or business person. Helpful tool for those who are keen to future-proof their careers."
—*Graham Southwell, National Director, Business Network International (BNI), New Zealand*

"Not only did *The Naked Career* reaffirm my capabilities, through its disciplined framework, I set about unlocking and realizing the keys to a successful and rewarding career journey within a dynamic changing industry. For those who are serious about taking a chance to develop their untapped potential, this is a fantastic interactive pathway that will give you the inner courage to rediscover and follow your passion. Start today!"
—*Andrew Laing, Travel Agent*

THE
Naked

CAREER

Your Journey to Emotional and Financial Fulfillment

STEPHEN CONWAY
and PAUL MEYER

TATE PUBLISHING, LLC

Printed in New Zealand with assistance from www.publishme.co.nz.

Published in the United States of America
by Tate Publishing, LLC
127 East Trade Center Terrace
Mustang, OK 73064
(888) 361–9473

ISBN: 1–5988625–4-5

ACKNOWLEDGEMENTS

Stephen would like to thank his mother Lyn for her support in so many ways and his brother Richard for keeping him on track. Also to indicate his appreciation for various mentors and teachers in his life, especially to Teena who prompted him to persevere. She had the foresight to see and advise when we only had one career product that there was a lot more yet to be done. So began the writing of a complete set of career stages.

To the various people who provided a spiritual sanctuary, helping me through my transition both emotionally and with their encouragement: Gail Nicholls, Lorraine Willmott, Barbara and Malcolm Dobbs, and Marjorie Rowe. To Richard Webster, for his advice and Angelina Weir, for inspiring me to write this book at the right time.

Also to thank Paul Meyer, back in 1995 for his respect and for both seeing and believing in my greater potential, at a time when all doors seemed closed. Most of all for giving of his time to my journey, with the sharing of his knowledge, to make it more meaningful and to help me grow. His support has been the mainstay in every subsequent project.

Paul has been influenced by so many encouraging people during his careers it is impossible to name and thank them all, but to say that it has been both rewarding and fulfilling to be associated with you all over the years.

He would like to specifically thank his parents May and Colin who have always believed in his potential and shown love and belief in all he undertook to do. Mum, your unconditional love has been unswerving and Dad you taught me "to always have a project on."

To Rosemary my beautiful wife, I thank you for your love, understanding and for our wonderful children, Gavin, Karen, Louise and Brendan. Without all their support and interesting career paths this book would never have become a reality.

Paul's first interest in writing was perhaps sparked by Rory Burke, who has become a good friend and mentor through this entire project. Thank you Rory, for your objective view point and intrigue about my zest and enthusiasm for life.

Finally I would like to thank Stephen who has been my challenge to see reach his full potential, now also as an author. Your determination, eye for detail and insistence that I meet deadlines has been invigorating. Together this book is an acknowledgement that two different life and career journeys can give rise to a valuable learning and educational tool to the world.

We are most grateful to Tate Publishing for recognizing the potential of this book. The encouragement from staff involved has been appreciated. We especially thank Trinity Tate for believing in us as authors, and Curtis Winkle for his professional editing guidance.

As Paul's mother taught him: "Life is like a drift of fallen snow, be weary how you tread it for every step will show." So please all love the life that you live and live the life that you love throughout all your careers.

CONTENTS

FOREWORD

I first met Paul and Stephen when I applied for a job they were recruiting. To bolster my CV, I enclosed a copy of a project management book I had written. I must have impressed Paul and Stephen because they have now burst into print themselves, however, I don't think I impressed them that much as I did not get the job!

With deregulation, outsourcing, off-shoring and automation the landscape of our working environment has changed forever. And with it the concept of a *job for life* is a thing of the past (even in Japan!). The reality is that most people are going to have many jobs or many careers in their lifetime. We therefore need to prepare ourselves and equip ourselves to be able to manage these career changes and make the most of these career opportunities as they arise. Herein lies the significant contribution of this book.

Having a comprehensive guidebook which has been drawn up by two experts will enable you to manage your career path to suit your life's journey, not the other way round, where you let your career path rule your life. This book outlines many practical methods to evaluate who you are and quantify what you want from life, so that you can take control of your career.

One of the best models for gaining an overview of where you are and where you are going is the *career life cycle.* The career life cycle shows how our life can be subdivided into a number of phases or stages as we progress from education to work, from apprenticeship to management, and from work to retirement.

The key to success is to manage each of these phases as a project and appreciate that each phase will come to an end, and therefore needs to be interlinked with the next phase. Once you accept that our lives are a series of stepping stones or building blocks, then you will appreciate why education and experience progressively pays dividends in later life. The career life cycle will also enable you to plan for redundancy and changing market forces, so you can reposition yourself to achieve a better lifestyle.

This book by Paul and Stephen will give you the confidence to take control of your career and enable you to strike a balance between career and income, achievement and lifestyle.

Rory Burke,
MSc Project Management from Henley Management College
Author
Lifestyle Entrepreneur

ABOUT THE AUTHORS

Stephen Conway has been on a life journey to discover his passion and like many young men was unsure of what he wanted to do after he left school. Stephen was the second son of a loving family. His father was a successful tradesperson, but sadly during Stephen's impressionable teenage years passed away after a long illness.

Stephen's early career years were in accounting, administration, customer services and the like. After many false starts in the 1980s he found himself in career transition and needing support during unemployment. This experience gave him a deeper understanding of life, and was a time of emotional and spiritual growth. During the 1990s he completed many training courses, which led to voluntary work, contract warehousing, recruiting and coaching.

In 1997 Stephen founded *"Career Navigators"* with Paul, to launch himself into business. This led to a passion for career development and to share his life experience with others. He has faced many career setbacks, as well as spiritual crises in the midst of change. He now sees his career as a lifelong journey, of which being an author, life and career coach, is but part of fulfilling his dreams and lifestyle aims.

With life being his teacher he now sees this book as sharing knowledge, wisdom and insights to help people from all walks of life integrate their career with personal growth. Then we can all have a better foundation in life for ourselves and others to use our talents and abilities to make a better world.

Paul Meyer has always had a passion for developing people to reach their full potential. In so doing he also develops and continues to achieve his stretch goals. An individual, who is now on the upper side of 50, Paul has enjoyed over 30 years of fun with his wife Rosemary as they have brought up 4 children. Paul probably followed his parents' family pattern, as he also was the eldest of 4 children.

His first career was banking and this conditioned him to get a qualification, accept transfers freely and take the traditional path to bank manager status. Were it not for his opportunity to take voluntary redundancy in 1989 he may still be a banker today.

In 1990 Paul chose private enterprise and has since been in business for himself, now specializing in taking the stress out of health and safety, management consulting and personal development. He has an interest in the early childhood industry and still strives to reach his full potential.

This book is a shared journey following his association with Stephen Conway and the foundation of *Career Navigators* back in 1997. May the readers gain insights into how they may choose a career that is fulfilling, fun and fits their journey to lifestyle freedom.

For the authors, *"The Naked Career"* completes a life mission to share their knowledge and wisdom and to inspire others. We all have lessons to learn in life, some of them very hard, but the essence that comes from our inner journey and spiritual gifts is ultimately expressed in the contribution we make to the world. We hope it helps you understand, recognize and move forward in your own unique life journey.

HOW TO USE THIS BOOK

The philosophy behind the book is that careers play a significant part in life's journey.

Our unique talents and abilities are uncovered progressively either directly or indirectly as a result of life's experiences. Through good personal career development, the reader will project confidence, discover the joy of fulfilling work and take actions that help him/her move towards their full potential. The theme in each chapter is basically to teach, reflect and take action, so that it is also a workbook. The graphics will assist learning as we often remember pictures better than we do words.

Some chapters have coaching questions. These are to prompt you to jot down ideas or encourage you to explore further. *(There are now many career resources available.)*

We may be able to think about or visualize what we want, but it does not belong to you until you write it down. Other sections have questionnaires or self-awareness tools to help you understand or monitor your present situation.

There are three different ways of looking at this book:

1. Read the book from beginning to end and use the tools along the way. This is suitable for people starting out on their career, in transition or considering a career change.

2. You may be happy in your work-life but looking for career enrichment and find yourself drawn or curious about certain sections in this book. If that is the case, you are bound to find something new or helpful. The rest of the book becomes a guide to be used as required. (e.g., *Life plan over the decades,* and *valuing your career charts*)

3. Simply use it as reference book. For example, if you are not coping with change, turn to an appropriate chapter for review and if necessary use some of the life tools.

Some of the tools in this book are challenging and may take some time to fully grasp. An example is the *career life cycle.* This is a reflective tool to help you see where you have been in terms of your career, and will also encourage you to project into the future. For some readers this may be hard to do. That is okay; just see this tool as being part of all the tools available in the career life journey and it will eventually take on a different meaning for you.

Overall the material in this book is to give you a snapshot of your life journey, which is different for each of us as we are all at different stages. The key is for you to find the right answer for yourself. We hope you will find it practical, real, and an opportunity to be reflective. Others will also see it as creative, perceptive and intuitive. However you view it, hopefully it will give you deeper meaning and purpose, to analyze issues and decisions in seeking answers and direction. The ultimate responsibility is yours as is what choices you make.

This book starts with an introduction to set the scene, and you will see why it can play an important part in your life. The following chapters will lead you on an amazing journey of exploration.

INTRODUCTION

Traditionally, career development has been associated with training while in a job, doing an apprenticeship or often climbing the ladder to more responsibility within an organization. Previously employers provided career training for promotion or you may have had a job until retirement. There has been a career paradigm shift in recent years where career development is primarily the responsibility of the individual. Employers are now driven to encourage personal development training to grow and retain employees. Today, due to the speed of change and globalization, it is a fact that most people will have many career and/or job changes in a lifetime. Some of these changes will be forced on us while others will be voluntary. Paul's son had around 18 jobs before he found his current career in locksmithing. In years gone by this may have been seen as a negative aspect to employment. This has helped prepare him for a suitable career where dealing with clients in many industry sectors is required.

Employee development is being affected by local, national and international influences.

In the local and international economies a large proportion of the workforce has less job security than before and temporary or short-term work is more common. Employment law and other government regulations, the high number of small business operations, low productivity and skill shortages are making it harder for business to meet employee's personal growth needs. Immigration has led to a wider diversity in the entry-level workforce. Many of these new entrants do not have any career development training.

Other changes in demography such as the middle-aging of the workforce and the growth in employment of women have brought about a greater demand for support services, convenient jobs and work/life balance for health and family concerns. Many will gain business experience on the job, and then leave to start enterprises of their own. Many women have a larger range of life skills and their goals and work styles differ. Mature workers will need training, re-education and new work assignments as well as to consider new life choices and careers. The aging population is bringing about pressure to increase the retirement age. In preparing people for a longer, diverse working life, career development plays a greater role together with lifestyle and financial planning. Periods of unemployment and redundancy have become common and early intervention to assist transition is necessary rather than leave it to market forces.

Information technologies and the internet are driving the pace of change through new ideas, knowledge and information. This means work will be organized in projects, doing multiple jobs at the same time and the product life-cycles will be shorter.

Career development now involves learning about the changing nature of work and how to practice and work with people to create more satisfying lives. It also means paid employment is only one facet of an individual's life or work and emphasizes the necessity for individuals to be their own life/career managers. So a career is coming to mean a lifelong journey consisting of many different jobs or roles, whether paid or unpaid.

The challenges in life today are not only to support yourself and to express yourself, but also to have the tools to cope with ongoing work and life transitions. One of the keys today is to know how to survive and grow in the midst of change. Career management training is essential both in terms of individual job satisfaction and to play a role in preparing a financial vehicle for wealth creation into the future.

The main implication of career development for the future is the recognition that we as humans are in a state of constant change both within ourselves and as a reaction to changes in our work environment. This will mean many different transitions as we progress through the career life cycle. As we get older, work and life balance become more important as we seek meaning and purpose in our lives. As people have job changes they are getting closer to understanding who they really are. Eventually, you reach a point where finding an environment where you feel comfortable to be yourself, becomes all-important. This is especially so as life tends to repeat itself if the transition has not been managed correctly the first time. In one sense if you are required to go to a low point the first time, any subsequent transitions can be passed through more quickly.

Traditional vocational guidance theory and practice has been primarily about helping people explore their interests, aptitudes and values. Often this involved various tests with professional assistance. The idea was to determine a best fit occupation and to try to match the job to the person, often falling back on what the person is good at doing or has done in the past. The next step being to provide information and develop a plan to obtain training or secure a job with the intention of working hard, climbing the ladder, and retiring at a set age. Perhaps receiving a gold watch for your loyalty. It assumed there would be a long-term career choice and did not take into account the constant need to change. The problem here is that what we are good at is not necessarily what we want to do, and this becomes frustrating later in life. A weakness of this vocational model was to match the job to the person rather than the job that meets the person's needs so they can see other possibilities for growth outside the square of the particular role. The world is now a faster changing place, so skills and values are more important in matching people to jobs.

The new set of beliefs, now practiced by many, is to know yourself well, believe in yourself and follow your heart. Simply focus on the journey, and accept that change brings with it new opportunities and learning that is lifelong. Here questions include what type of situations, organizations, environments, work roles and arrangements will suit you. While permanent, secure jobs are scarcer, at the same time this acknowledges there are more interesting and rewarding opportunities, although in less long-term permanent form. Career development is necessary so people can identify these opportunities quickly.

We now need knowledge workers who are lifelong learners who can respond and adapt to change. This is because of the changing work roles. These different categories include: full / part time employment, contracting, consulting, self-employment and entrepreneurship. Many people work a variety of jobs to build a sustainable income. Much work today is project based and this demands a high level of self-knowledge, self-confidence and adaptability, which are also career development skills, that can be learned.

The expectation now is that careers change more frequently than past traditions dictated. Often in the business environment today, employers are reluctant to engage people who do not have clear goals and ambitions, which is a key career development skill. As a result, employees need to be prepared to pursue personal ambitions that require changes of employer. Many youth today are not sure how to make good career decisions. Even after graduating, some are not clear what they want to do and end up in unrelated jobs. Similarly, many small to medium business have no formal employee training programmes nor individual and development or human resource services. This results in many adults making career choices with little focus and direction, often without having learned the necessary career management skills to succeed and then they find themselves changing employment without proper preparation.

Work habits and attitudes strongly influence early adult earnings, so work behaviors need to be emphasized as much as job skills. Today many employment opportunities are to be found in small businesses. While they may be able to use employee skills easily, if you're looking for job security, that is entirely dependent upon the success of the firm and demand for their products and services. Self-reliance evolves out of these career management skills.

The challenge is to help youth and adults learn how to choose wisely and commit to ongoing self-improvement for the rewards of satisfaction and self-fulfillment. In the future, individuals must seek training that equips them to take responsibility for their own career development. No longer can personal and career concerns be separated, as one drives the other. They need to become directors as well as actors in life and career choices. This means being focused on what they want and taking action, which helps them feel more in control and capable of achieving their dreams.

Acquiring personal career development skills increases the likelihood of workplace success. It also improves the chances of selection and advancement in employment opportunities. From a personal point of view, the increased self-confidence is likely to lead to success in relationships, family and the community. In our society today much emphasis has been placed on academic, business management and technical skills, but not so for the career skills that people need to cope with changing workplaces or when they have more than one career in a lifetime. This is due to the fact that people's financial and personal growth needs change as they progress through life.

Career development for everyone requires continual learning rather than an occasional counseling or coaching session when things go wrong. Thus the growth in business, performance and life coaching, indicating work life concerns in society. Career development is about using tools for managing your career and work changes throughout life.

The changes in the work environment are making it increasingly difficult to have a secure career plan with one employer. Organizations need people who can learn quickly, solve problems and come up with creative ideas for sustainable competitive advantage. Managers and employers will want to build skills and confidence to ensure ongoing employment for growth and promotion. If people feel unappreciated, and don't get the rewards they are worthy of, they are more likely to move on.

The outcome of career development is that your inner

satisfaction is just as important as your outer success in the world. It is about the personal leadership skills required to take action, take risks and learn new skills, to help navigate the work environment.

Coaching for further development will more likely meet the needs of the changing global market place as people search for different income streams, are more likely at some point to go into business, and will need to adapt to periodic cycles of upskilling.

The number of dual career couples will continue to increase and people will also have to concern themselves with childcare and elderly care. This means the individual will truly be on their own in developing a career. They will need support as a new style of boundaryless career, (e.g. several different part-time jobs or other combinations of work life) is emerging. This can lead to accepting lower income compared to the benefits and security of a stable career path with a single full-time employer. The onus is on those looking for work to find the employment opportunities that are out there or in many cases create opportunities of their own through self-employment.

As work circumstances change, learning new things, skills, techniques and relationships become part of managing your life. Interestingly, many great leaders have had little formal education yet have achieved great success through adopting the right attitude and motivation. Normally they gain knowledge by "doing," and now have a competitive edge in their particular job or profession. It is recognized that these skills came from continued learning, both formally and informally.

In summary, the nature of career development is such that in the future it is likely to finally be acknowledged as good for the advancement of the individual and society. Better use will have to be made of the limited human resources available, and people in future will seek more balance and freedom in their lives.

Perhaps the time is coming when we will review our career and work life progress annually, rather than wait for circumstances to force a change. In this way you will be able to determine whether your current position is supporting your short and long-term ambitions. So the career becomes the "financial vehicle" to take you through life where you are able to use and express your full range of talents and abilities.

The concept of career development is still not recognized by many employers, as it is new and evolving. Many are still afraid they will lose staff and this becomes a barrier. However, the reverse side of the coin is the difficulty in keeping staff who increasingly want better job satisfaction and to work in an environment that meets their values. The quality of life in terms of balance, health and wellbeing is becoming all-important, as is often expressed by the saying work smarter not harder.

The benefits from career development are both tangible (financial) and intangible (personal growth). Those who do some form of career development tend to invest more energy into their workplace. For the unemployed it could shorten the period out of work and in many cases prevent it from happening again or so regularly. It all links in well with life, business and performance coaching, career and financial planning, budgeting, building lifelong skills, developing one's potential as an employee, leader or entrepreneur, and will ultimately bring about more satisfaction and a feeling of inner success.

This book is about stripping away all the barriers to career fulfillment. It breaks down a career into the different components of what makes us who we are as we progress through life. Just like a rough diamond is said to be someone who can be molded into a shining example to others, so too can careers be molded to fit one's lifestyle. Throughout the book, each chapter has a symbol of a diamond, to signify the value placed on each life to be a shining success in their individual careers.

This book seeks to answer the question, "Do you have a career for life?" Whether you work to live or live to work, the information in the following chapters will challenge you to think differently about your career. It offers tools that will assist in your career growth and inspire you to greater achievements. Along the way remember you must have fun and create your future.

CHAPTER 1

Are You Playing Hide & Seek?

As children we learn to discover by curiosity. When we mature our curiosity is stifled by our past conditioning, frequently associated with work and relationships. Often we hide under the security of a perceived safe place. When that safe haven is removed, our tendency is to seek out another safe place for fear of taking risk and/or ending up a failure.

These safe places are often disguised as job security, like following a career similar to our parents.' Yet, to seek out our hidden career potential, we must search outside the obvious.

As we progress in life we experience many transitions. These can be foundation changes after such events as redundancy, bereavement, career redirection, etc. You cannot go through life without any transitions, as they are often the ending of a phase and the beginning of another.

To seek out the ideal career path usually involves a lot of soul searching with no one person to direct you. If you are hiding from your career potential, it will only be released when you discover the inner courage to follow your passion. Your passion is recognized only when the confidence to "pass I on" is unshakeable in the path of any adversity. Many people will be constantly challenged to re-assess where they are going in life in a rapidly changing world. In fact right through their life journey. It is the journey that gives us the experience. Sustaining motivation and drive ensures chosen career opportunities can be realized.

Are you hiding from the choice to have the lifestyle you deserve simply because you are afraid? Careers are the catalyst in life for the freedom in your lifestyle to be, have, and become what you are capable of becoming.

We seek freedom through:
- Mind
- Health
- Fulfillment
- Fun
- Leisure
- Beliefs
- Love
- Relationships
- Wealth

This book is about being driven to make the changes that will give you lifestyle freedom through the best career opportunities.

It seems inevitable as we progress, that life will present challenges on many fronts. These can be social, economic, technological and / or financial. While these can create stress, they help also in the search to identify with some life purpose. This can be revealed through personal development and life skills. It is only after crystallising one's life purpose

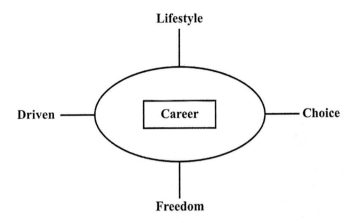

that we can move towards real freedom and contribute our full range of talents to the world.

Many of us have dreams and desires that are never accomplished simply because we don't take the time to acknowledge who we want to be. The amazing reality is that once this knowledge is gained, all things are possible and we no longer need to hide. At this point we can express and find ways to support ourselves freely. This way we are not playing hide and seek with the reality we must face.

CHAPTER 2

It's Fun to Work

They say families that play together stay together. We spend so much time at work that it's important to have some fun along the way. This in turn makes us great people to be around.

Happy people are productive people.

When you are happy at work you are:

- Inspired
- More fulfilled
- More creative
- More contented
- Able to find solutions
- Looking for challenges
- More productive
- More motivated
- Energised
- Healthier

Overall you feel better about yourself and project a happy attitude in your work and in relationships with fellow employees and clients.

A happy, fun-loving team of people will always outperform the disgruntled, grumpy, negative team.

What are some recent examples of fun you had in your work environment?

If examples do not come to mind quickly, you must question whether you are having fun at work.

They say that you smile and the world smiles with you. It is so simple and costs nothing.

When did you last have a great laugh about something at work?

How many times do you smile in a day?

Are you doing work that makes you feel good about yourself?

Are you a Smiler?
Some
Members
Initiate
Laughter in
Employment
Regularly

Understand that your career journey will have both difficult and fun times. All are necessary, but laughter often goes a long way to diluting a difficult situation. Laughter is a sign of a happy person, so, when projected genuinely, it will attract to you positive environments, which will make career activities more rewarding and successful.

Fun brings an extra dimension into your life that makes other things possible and creates better relationships.

There have been many studies about laughter. Paul recalls a life-changing experience about laughter in his first work place. At this engineering firm his first manager, Des, a very happy chap, was well liked and respected by all the staff. He was a bit of an entertainer and could always share a funny joke naturally. One day he took Paul aside and said, "It is important that you develop your own style of laughter." These words of wisdom have echoed through Paul's career years, endorsing to him that fun must be an element to enjoying life and work. Des sadly died in the prime years of his career as the result of an accident, but his legacy to have fun in the work place lives on.

Common views are that it relieves stress and releases a chemical that relaxes the mind. Laughter is generally all positive and happy. It is difficult to laugh about something negative.

Fun-loving people have a **F**riendly
Unique
Nature

A fun-loving person has a high self-esteem and projects this confidence to communicate in all circles. They also have the ability to laugh at themselves when circumstances permit. They are nice to be around and make great employers and employees.

Fun
Undermines
Negativity and allows us to be happy within ourselves.

You spend a large part of your life at work, so it's important you enjoy it.

What would you like to do different that would give more fun in your life and work

• Today?

• This week?

• This month?

A simple test is to ask when did you last tell a joke?

If you are in a career that you enjoy, then you will have more fun at work.

CHAPTER 3

The Tip of the Iceberg

It has been said that most people don't utilise any more than 10% of their natural talents and abilities. This untapped potential can be likened to the submerged part of an iceberg. One-ninth can be seen above the waterline and eight-ninths lie unseen but have the force to make major changes.

What we mean by above the line is the attitudes, beliefs and skills that are getting you what you presently enjoy in life. The link is to get what you want. Many people are getting what they need, but not what they want.

Your potential lies beneath the surface just like with the iceberg. The current and flow on the eight-ninths controls where the one-ninth (above the surface) goes. This untapped potential does not have to wait for a disaster to have its power released.

Think about the sinking of a great ship like the titanic. What was seen was only the tip of the iceberg. The real potential to change lay below the surface of the sea. In fact, it ripped open the hull of an unsinkable ship. The change was so catastrophic, that the ship sank with the loss of many lives.

Our hidden potential is within our talents and abilities that have not yet been realised.

Unfortunately, the greatest limitations to us achieving our potential are those which are self-imposed. What will force you to search for your hidden potential? Such forces include redundancy, retirement, job and life dissatisfaction, financial changes, health challenges, difficult relationships, moving locations, feelings of rejection, and a lack of purpose or direction. All of these things can make you feel like you are being sucked into a whirlpool if you don't grip onto something.

We have to recognize that our potential is unlimited and that we can choose a career that will develop us into who we want to be. Normally you will not be successful in your resolve to develop your untapped potential until you have accepted that it is a journey of progressively setting worthwhile predetermined personal goals.

Often people associate success with wealth and other

tangible items, but in fact, true peace of mind comes about when the inner-self believes what the outer-self can achieve. To utilise your potential, you need to have a strong, positive self-image and not be set back by the barriers and frustrations associated with achieving any personal and career goals.

As Henry Ford once said, *"If you think you can or you think you can't you are right."*

If you think yourself as a failure, you will fail no matter how hard you consciously try to succeed. If you have a low self image, then this will produce negative attitudes and hamper the development of personal leadership, and you won't be able to forge ahead in whatever career you may be in or about to undertake. Self-image revolves around starting with a strong self-worth and not allowing other people's importance to put you down.

A common affirmation used by successful people to overcome other influences is:

I am important and so is everybody else, but I will not allow other people's importance to put me down.

Once we realise we have untapped potential, we are in a position to make choices that use our talents and abilities effectively in a career. In our younger years, life seems to be filled with many choices. For example, education, work, careers, relationships, etc. Career choices can narrow, particularly as we mature in life and impose self-disbelief. (e.g., "I am too old for that.")

We cannot advance until we dare to take a chance. Taking a chance means running the risk of possible failure, real hurt. It takes courage. Courage isn't a gift; courage is a decision. Courage is that scary emotion that motivates us to make the right decision.

Be courageous in making your career choices.

Choices are important for the following reasons:

1. Choice is a talent that must be developed. The power of choice affects outcomes. You must accept that if you are reluctant to make choices because of fear or failure, then you may choose to play it safe and miss that very experience that could utilise your full talents and abilities.

2. You must choose for yourself, accepting self-responsibility and that who you are today is in direct proportion to the decisions you have made in the past. This allows you the choice to make the change and accept the past as something that forms a natural part of you, whether there are negative or positive experiences in your life.

3. Once you have accepted this responsibility, you need to understand that choice determines the consequences. Therefore, if you elect to take an action or a direction, those consequences will be directly in proportion to the actions you have taken.

Freedom of choice is your natural gift. Therefore, understand that your risk threshold is an important component in making choices and decisions. You can liken risk to various forms of financial investments you might make. Some people are happy to have their funds invested in an income asset, where there is a regular income. Others prefer to invest in equities or shares where the risks may be higher but the returns may be greater. The same applies to changes we make in our career. Often the most successful career people take risks. The entrepreneur, however, does calculate these risks and gathers the appropriate information to ensure the decisions that are made are based on good, sound facts. There always becomes a point where a decision must be made whether to use your untapped potential or leave it hidden, as in the iceberg example, sitting below the surface.

COACHING QUESTION:

What are some things that your life is asking you to do, or hinting at, that you are not doing and putting off? These are a part of your untapped potential.

CHAPTER 4

The Significance of Your Career

Most of the first part of life (up to 25 years in our example), is spent learning and educating for the income-earning years. This is represented from age 25–70, which is 35% of the time available in life. During these income-earning years, 14% of the time is available for work (in our example 7am to 6pm), and the remaining 21% for eating, sleeping and other life-balancing activities.

This 14% often runs the other 86% of life. Your career choices and/or successes and failures govern the life you live. It represents only 14% of your life period from age 0–100 when working for 45 years on average from 7am to 6pm, 5 days per week with 3 weeks annual leave in our example.

Effectively, the first stage of one's life is learning, educating and preparing for the career/earning years. This can be up to 25% of one's life period depending on time starting work.

Once the decision to step into a career has been made, this often influences many other factors in life, including

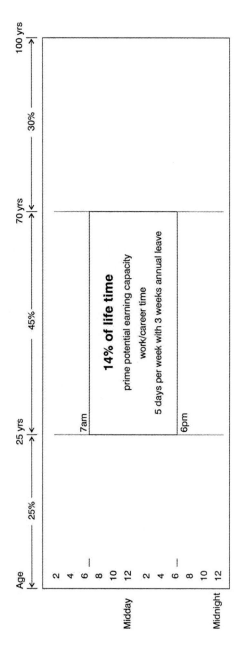

14% Working career (age 25 to 70 years - working 7am to 6pm)

30% Sleep/Rest (average 7.2 hours per day)

56% Eating/Living/Relaxation/Education

100% Lifes total time "on the earth".

Why focusing on your career is important to success in life?

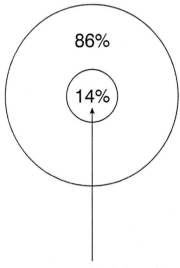

Get it right because it affects the
other 86% of your "living" time.

quality of relationships, spending / saving capacity, further education and future prospects for growth. In fact, our work environment conditions us the earlier we start work. That is before our own unique characteristics have been developed. The significance of your career comes from understanding how such a small part of life (14% of total time) dominates the largest part of time remaining in life (86%).

Your first 25 years (the prime learning years) are often influenced by the careers of parents, guardian or extended family groups. The quality of life from 70 onwards or whatever time one's career concludes, is directly proportionate to how you use your potential in the career years.

Reflecting on this example, the following career questions can be asked for each age group:

Age 0–25   Have you prepared adequately?

25-70   Are you in the career of your choice?

70+   Are these continuing to be the best years of your life?

If you are happy in your career, it will tend to support the other areas in your life, and boost your self-esteem and confidence. On the other hand, if you are fulfilled in all the other areas of your life, it will in turn assist your career potential.

Key ideas:

1. Prepare adequately with appropriate education and training

2. Ensure career choices support wellbeing.

3. Manifest wealth to give independence throughout life.

CHAPTER 5

Comfort Zones

Understanding that managed levels of discomfort are how you achieve personal growth will prepare you for discovering your full career potential. We are in a perpetual state of discomfort. What causes this discomfort is a self-awareness that develops with maturity and time, namely wisdom.

What is discomfort? The effects of discomfort can be mental, emotional and physical.

Sometimes you are good at what you do, but the environment causes discomfort. Just because you are good at something, it is not necessarily what you should do.

Many years ago the following was shared in a development group:

> *I used to have a comfort zone where I knew I couldn't fail.*
> *The same four walls and busy work were really more like jail.*
> *I longed so much to do some things I'd never done before.*
> *But stayed inside my "comfort zone" and paced the same old floor.*
>
> *I said it didn't matter that I wasn't doing much.*

I said I didn't care for things like diamonds, furs and such.
I claimed to be so busy with things inside the zone
But deep down inside I longed for something special of my own.

I couldn't let life go by just watching others win!
I held my breath and stepped outside to let the change begin!
I took a step and with new strength I'd never felt before,
I kissed my "comfort zone" good-bye and closed and locked the door.

If you are in a 'comfort zone' and afraid to venture out,
Remember that all winners were at one time filled with doubt.
A step or two and words of praise can make your dreams come true.

Greet your future with a smile. Success is there for you.

Source: anonymous

Change causes discomfort because of uncertainty. Routines are the basis for stable living which give you certainty and purpose. For example, work is often the prime purpose for one's life/existence as it fills in time (or makes it go faster).

You very seldom recognize change in yourself, but often find that others see these changes with more ease looking from the outside in, rather than the inside out.

However, at some stage you feel different about things, which reflects from a change in your comfort zone. For example, stepping onto a suspended boat in a swinging cradle being transferred from land to water will feel very uncomfortable the first time, but once the manoeuvre is completed and you are safely on the water there is a new comfort.

When we set new challenges and decide to change, there is always personal growth. To enjoy your career journey, you need to be comfortable with who you are. Understanding that periods of discomfort when well managed are critical to personal growth enables you to move forward at your desired pace. The key concept to accept is that the cycle of life has periods of intense discomfort which, if managed effectively, convert to wisdom. On the other hand, they can indicate challenges ahead, so these signals are best recognized and acted upon.

Personal growth can be linked to the change from the old comfort zone to a new comfort zone. This can be illustrated as follows:

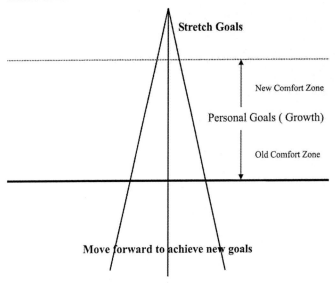

Stretch Goals

New Comfort Zone

Personal Goals (Growth)

Old Comfort Zone

Move forward to achieve new goals

COACHING QUESTIONS:

Picture for yourself where you have made a move from one job to another (or different type of work).

1. What were you previously comfortable doing?

2. What has changed in your new comfort zone?

Often, people don't have stretch goals and are not comfortable with where they are in their life. Setting smaller goals/steps ensures personal growth can still be achieved, but at a slower pace.

A good idea is to set goals in 3 stages. For example, have a minimum achievement, an ideal level and a dream goal. If you use wages as an example, there is a minimum to cover basics, an ideal may be basics plus savings, and a dream could be basics plus savings and holidays.

The only way to change your comfort zones is to set goals and take action to achieve them over a predetermined time frame.

CHAPTER 6

The Changing Nature of Careers

The nature of careers is changing significantly, with many terms used to describe these differences. Such terms used include:

- Dual Careers
- Composite / Portfolio Careers
- Multiple Careers
- Complementary Careers
- Patchwork Careers
- Entrepreneurial Careers

Your future is bright if you really want it to be, but this will be influenced by your career choices. A career has five distinct meanings, which can be defined as follows:

- Career as advancement
- Career as a profession
- Career as a lifelong sequence of jobs
- Career as a sequence of role-related experiences
- Career as a lifelong sequence of work attitudes and behaviours

Traditional career development was associated with advancement and promotion, often over years of loyalty. Today, this definition must include other types of career goals that you might have for personal development, also. You can consider a career as any lifelong sequence of jobs, regardless of whether it is inside or outside a profession. This is a summarized definition of the meaning of a career. The actual definition has evolved over many years and the original references come from the following sources.

• Hall, D. T. & Hall, F. S. (1976) "Career development: how organisations put their fingerprints on people," in L. Dyer (ed), *Careers in Organisations,* New York State School of Industrial and Labor Relations, Cornell University, pp 15

• Thomas, A. B. (1981) "The career graph: a tool for mid-career development," Personnel Review, vol 10, no 3, p 19

• Rudman, Richard. (1999) *Human Resources Management in New Zealand,* 3rd edn, Addison Wesley Longman, Auckland, pp 473–4

Careers are usually the income-earning vehicles, but often one career may not produce adequate money. Your career is an influential part of your journey through life, which at different stages involves consideration of your relationships and development of yourself.

One of these changes is being reflected in *dual careers.* There are two interpretations of this. One type is two people in a relationship, both with careers. Example: A company director in a business with the other party following a medical career. The other type of dual career, also known as a *composite or portfolio* career, is where one person follows two or more careers at the same time. Example: A composite career where one career is computer programming and the other is tutoring in another field.

Multiple careers can involve a number of ventures of which different talents are needed. Often this involves a combination of income methods. For example, one career as an owner/stakeholder in a childcare centre. Another career as a health and safety advisor with performance remuneration, and another as a telemarketer, receiving income as an employee.

Many careers have developed with a common thread and often complement one another. These *complementary careers* prove successful because of their associated nature. For example, a landscaper who designs and produces plans for new gardens may also be a salesperson for ready-made lawns.

Patchwork careers often develop through necessity to obtain an income stream from various sources. These could be either several part-time jobs/careers and/or a combination of various business interests. For example, a person in early retirement may decide to take up green keeping because of their interest in golf but spend half a day consulting to a past employer, and one day a week in a family business or like.

Finally, the *entrepreneurial career* develops when ambitions are to create wealth and make this the income-earning vehicle, often establishing or purchasing passive income streams. This could stem from network marketing, property portfolios or establishing a successful business that can be managed and run remotely. Entrepreneurs enjoy duplicating themselves and the business models they create.

COACHING QUESTIONS:

• Which type of career can you see yourself doing in the future?

• How will this enable you to use more of your potential?

CHAPTER 7

Can't Find It

Have you found yourself in the position of not being able to find yourself, in your career that is. Yes, often people wake up to the fact that they are going to work purely through habit and need to earn money to live. The quality of life at this point is usually boring, unstimulating and with little prospect for career progression.

This chapter is about "finding it" through the progression of our changing careers.

By using the career future indicator, you can learn how you are coping in your career.

You can find yourself.

Career Future Indicator (CFI)

This is to evaluate whether enriching your present career or planning a career change is more appropriate.

Instructions: Answer the following questions and **circle the letter** (A, B or C) that best reflects your view today. Then measure how you are doing on the C.F.I. evaluator.

1. How satisfied are you in your present career?

    A. I'm right where I want to be.

    B. Some days it feels fine but I have increasing times of doubt.

    C. I find it hard to go to work each day.

2. How much do you use your talents and abilities?

    A. 80–90% of the time.

    B. 50–80% of the time

    C. Less than 50% of the time

3. How is your present health in relation to your work and wellbeing?

    A. I am always enthusiastic and have energy for my work.

    B. I occasionally have tension /anxiety headaches but haven't needed to take days off.

    C. I have had over a week off in the last 6 months when I had difficulty coping with my responsibilities at work and /or home.

4. Is your present work achieving your personal career aspirations?

    A. I am very happy with my achievements in life.

    B. I have been meaning to write down my career goals but my life is too busy.

    C. I have always been wondering what my career aspirations are.

5. What is the rate of progress in your career/work?

A. I am happy and continually meet new challenges.

B. It is hard to progress in my career.

C. There are no opportunities for me to progress.

6. Is your present work/career environment stimulating?

A. I love to go to work everyday.

B. I don't get on with people around me.

C. I just don't thrive in this environment

7. Have you thought about changing your career or work?

A. I know if I make changes, I could further enrich my career.

B. I have applied for other positions outside my career but always seem to come second.

C. I'm afraid to change my career.

8. How committed are you to career change?

A. I would like a career change within the next 12 months.

B. I am yet to decide whether I am ready for change.

C. I will only change if the money is better.

9. How committed are you to career enrichment?

A. I have always believed my full potential can be achieved in my present career.

B. I need to investigate what opportunities I have to enrich my career.

C. I am not expecting any career enrichment.

10. What do you understand career change involves?

    A. Making a greater investment in myself.

    B. Focus solely on retraining in a different field.

    C. Changing jobs.

11. Are you in the right career?

    A. My work enhances my personality

    B. I have to suppress parts of my personality.

    C. My personality is better suited to a different kind of work.

12. How do you view change?

    A. I see change as an opportunity for fulfillment.

    B. I see change as neutral, i.e. neither good nor bad.

    C. I have some fear about change.

Write your % score here ☐

Time Log — Hours Spent Each Day

	TOTAL	Mon	Tue	Wed	Thur	Fri	Sat	Sun
Sleep								
Relaxation								
Family Time								
Hygiene/Dress/Meals								
Travel								
Work								
Hobbies								
Committee Meetings								
Social								
Church								
Housework								
Garden								
Watching TV								
Other								
Hours Available	168	24	24	24	24	24	24	24

Your Career Score Analysis

Over 70%

The higher your score, the more likely you will benefit from considering career development rather than a total career change. Look for ways to progress in your present career.

50% -69%

In this mid range, a career change may be necessary to ensure you fully use your talents and abilities and capture your personality traits. Consider options for careers that will best suit your attributes and skills.

Under 50%

The lower your score, the more likely you need to make personal changes to advance your career opportunities. This includes clear personal goals and knowing how these can be achieved in your work/career environment.

Now that you have evaluated how you are coping in your present career, it is timely to look at the reasons for your score. These can be summarised in the word COPE.

Climate
Organisation
People
Environment

Your pathway to a successful career/work is influenced by all these factors. If you can't find the right climate, organisation, people and environment, your potential will be stifled. Let's talk about each of these in turn.

Climate includes the natural forces that surround you but which you have no direct control over. They can be negative or positive. For example, a friendly, relaxed attitude with people enjoying their work activities is positive. On the other hand, it can be a tense, unwelcoming place without feeling. This being negative. A good climate has a feel-good factor, in other words you want to be there and go back to it.

Organisation is the industry sector, firm or employer, structure and actual place of work. Ultimately, to feel part of the organisation, its surroundings will be a natural extension of yourself. Are you in the organisation that brings out the best in you? Is your working style in harmony with the organisation? Conflicts and clashes in these areas will not see you coping and eventually will create high levels of stress.

People is about morale, leadership and the way in which you are supported and treated from new recruit to mature employee. This is often the greatest reason why staff leave a place of work. Similarly, a good attitude toward people will encourage longevity of service.

Are you with the right people? Do you know what people are right for you? A firm that encourages personal growth for its people usually values people assets.

Environment is the physical features in the workplace, from furniture decor to actual premises. Is the environment for your career the place of your choice? Is the transport to and from work convenient and have you the location or view you want?

Take control of your career future and link your passion to the climate, organisation, people and environment.

CHAPTER 8

I Don't Know

In the context of careers, the "I don't know" can be hidden in your career traps and conditioning. Let's see how these can affect our thinking.

There are messages or beliefs that we pick up from the environment around us which influence decisions we make about our life and career.

Indicate the following statements or beliefs you identify with:

☐ 1. Parents know what is best.

☐ 2. A job that pays well will make you happy.

☐ 3. Other people are in charge.

☐ 4. There is one perfect job for you.

☐ 5. If you choose a stable industry you will have a secure future.

☐ 6. Just be happy you have got a job.

☐ 7. Give loyal service and you will be rewarded.

☐ 8. A square peg in a round hole (or a round peg in a square hole).

☐ 9. What do you want to leave a good job like that for?

☐ 10. An unstable work history is bad for you.

☐ 11. If you have qualifications you should have no trouble getting a job.

☐ 12. It's too late to change.

☐ 13. As long as you do a good job there will be a place for you.

☐ 14. Career rebuilding stuff is only for the well educated.

☐ 15. All I want is a job.

☐ 16. I'm too busy to look at what I really want.

Taking Action:

Can you think of any others that influence you today? For example: Don't talk to strangers.

☐ Are they your own thoughts?
Or
☐ Did they come from other people?

Who said those things to you?

Do you now believe them to be ☐ true or

☐ false?

To move forward in career change and transition, we have to let go of old expectations and attitudes that stop us from having what we really want.

Write in the career traps and conditioning that you now wish to let go of.

For example: Too old to change–loyal service–perfect job–not qualified

We can replace those things we learned, that no longer work for us.

It is often during the bad times or transition period that these attitudes are tested in order to gain inner strength and move forward.

By developing an inner strength, we gain the courage to stand alone and move towards taking risks and choices in our life and career. These risks and choices are related to acceptance that we have unlimited potential.

CHAPTER 9

Managing the Information Revolution

Are your career options affected by this?

With the speed of change we are faced with accepting, technology is advancing at an ever-increasing pace. New technology is a double-edged sword. Traditional human functions are being replaced with technology, and this is creating new career opportunities.

If you have not been brought up with a computer in your household, you may be at a disadvantage to those who treat the computer as their daily business/household tool. Self-management of the information revolution certainly starts with acceptance that change is constant.

Nineteeth century careers were shaped by the industrial revolution and specific tasks associated with clearly defined roles that met a particular function. Work in the twenty-first century now depends on the ability to process vast amounts of information on very tight deadlines, just to achieve results that enhance an organisation's value and effectiveness. Information needs to be processed rapidly. Look how spamming has challenged emailing.

Strategies for handling the information revolution

1. Accept it as an indication of progress.

2. Know yourself, so you can use the information in the right way.

3. Select learning techniques to handle information.

4. Reduce the clutter.

5. Be flexible and willing to change. Simply have a go.

6. Consciously plan ahead and you will absorb new information easily.

7. Use global systems to search for relevant information.

There are many different ways of learning with technology, and through this we find better ways to do things. The huge knowledge gained in our health and education sectors has lead to information overload for many.

Technology gives us the ability to handle and process masses of information, and this has lead to new types of career opportunities. For example: forms of research, publishing and marketing via the internet.

A true test of whether you are taking advantage of the information revolution is to ask whether you can operate all the functions on your remote TV, your mobile phone, your microwave or a palm-held organiser.

If you don't, do you know someone who does?

The following **coaching questions** will help you determine how well you are managing the information revolution.

COACHING QUESTIONS

These days, change and new information always create new opportunities. List some of the new opportunities you have seen created in the last twelve months by the revolution of new information.

The only thing you can control is how you react and what opportunities you can create for yourself. Write down a new career opportunity you have thought of in the last twelve months but not acted upon.

Why has this idea/opportunity not happened so far?

What would you like to do about it?

CHAPTER 10

The Changing Global Workplace

The changing global workplace is being brought about by technological, economic and social changes. This is affecting the way that work is distributed throughout the world. Information and technology will continue to influence the structures we work with.

Individuals will need to take responsibility for their careers to gain full advantage of the global workplace. Intermingled with social and technological changes are the ongoing economic cycles, which include boom and gloom times.

These states can be seen in the following cycles:

In the social cycle, we revolve around the life span of our population. Nowadays youth are exposed to international travel and other global issues through media and modern communications. This gives worldwide exposure and influences that are across many countries and cultures. While searching for identity, the expectation is that overseas trends will affect the way you think and feel about yourself. Then

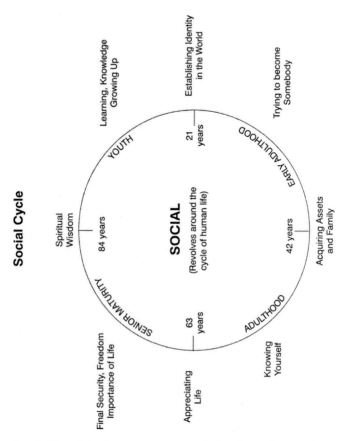

Social Cycle

SOCIAL
(Revolves around the
cycle of human life)

Learning, Knowledge
Growing Up

Establishing Identity
in the World

Trying to become
Somebody

YOUTH

EARLY ADULTHOOD

21 years

Spiritual
Wisdom

84 years

42 years

Acquiring Assets
and Family

SENIOR MATURITY

ADULTHOOD

63 years

Final Security, Freedom
Importance of Life

Appreciating
Life

Knowing
Yourself

in adulthood is the acceptance to do business internationally and have social circles that are in all parts of the world. There is now a freedom of choice to travel and experience careers in many countries. Also affecting careers are the changes to the traditional family structure. One partner is not always now the prime income earner.

There will always be economic cycles as changes take place in business, markets and governments. There are definite periods that affect the income levels dependent

68

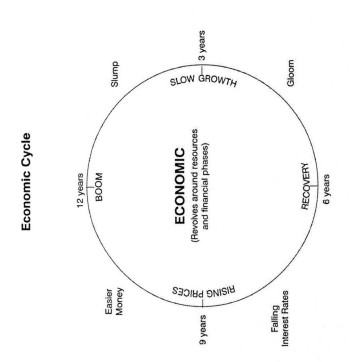

Economic Cycle

ECONOMIC
(Revolves around resources and financial phases)

SLOW GROWTH — 3 years

Slump

Gloom

BOOM — 12 years

RECOVERY — 6 years

Easier Money

RISING PRICES — 9 years

Falling Interest Rates

on growth and less buoyant times. Different skill levels for changing industries also cause skill shortages in some areas and creation of new jobs or careers in new fields.

The technology cycle has shown rapid change since the late 1990's and early 2000's.

Communication technology is a great example where the whole world is the workplace, not just an office or factory. This also means new ideas are spread rapidly and change is instant in many cases.

Career navigation is the interception of the set of cir-

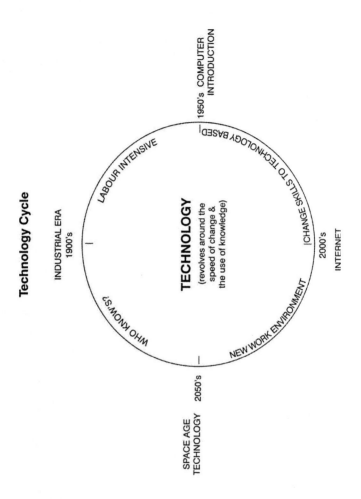

Technology Cycle

INDUSTRIAL ERA
1900's

LABOUR INTENSIVE

1950's COMPUTER
INTRODUCTION

CHANGE SKILLS TO TECHNOLOGY BASED

TECHNOLOGY
(revolves around the
speed of change &
the use of knowledge)

2000's
INTERNET

NEW WORK ENVIRONMENT

WHO KNOW'S?

SPACE AGE
TECHNOLOGY
2050's

cumstances that drive career change. The changes in the social, economic and technology cycles overlap so that one affects the other. This link can be illustrated as follows:

All these circumstances are constantly in a state of change, just like the universe.

Think of the changes in the world over the last century.

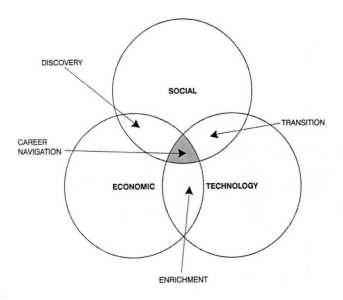

Our ancestors 100 years ago learned in a lifetime what we can now read in one newspaper. Imagine how much change we will see in the future given the availability of information and the speed of change. Think about the global link with the internet.

How are you placed as a result of the changing global workplace? Make a statement under each of the following headings:

1. Social (e.g., at age 46 confident with my inner-self but building wealth for retirement.)

2. Economic (e.g., after economic recovery interest rates low. Plan career for future boom times.)

3. Technology (e.g., now computer literate but need to develop internet skills for future work.)

Now let's look at the different attributes that are emerging as we change from the traditional type of employee to a new breed of employee.

Traditional employees were more likely to demand long-term job security. They tended to believe employers were responsible for career growth. Often they were less satisfied with their jobs, but stayed because they didn't know anything else. These employees often believed that changing jobs was damaging to their career. They tended to define loyalty as a tenure. The past traditional employee viewed work as an opportunity for income, not necessarily as a place where they could achieve personal growth and attainment of lifelong goals.

Now as we progress in the twenty-first century, the new breed of employees are more likely to reject job security as a driver of commitment. They are now tending to take personal responsibility for career growth and work to their own plan. Therefore, navigation of such a plan is a key ingredient to the successful emerging employees. The new type of employees are more satisfied with their jobs and believe that changing jobs often is part of growth. While they do give loyalty to an employer during a period of contract engagement, they tend to define loyalty as an accomplishment. Their view of work is as a choice to achieve personal satisfaction and lifelong goals that are fulfilling to them as complete people.

What type of employee are you? A traditional employee or a new breed of employee?

Write your thoughts:

The key aspect of the new breed of employee is that they see productivity as the key ingredient to the employer. In other words, what specific benefits can this bring to an employer to help them achieve their organisational goals?

Before moving ahead to navigate your plan, take time to define what you believe would be your definition of productivity. You will need to be as specific as possible, using measurable output-orientated terms.

List below in order of priority the six most important productive things you do, with number one being the most valuable and profitable.

1. _____

2. _____

3. _____

4. _____

5. _____

6. _____

This is used to list what you think your priorities are to achieve optimum productivity in either self-employment or an employment opportunity.

Now that you have had a look at what productivity means to you and prioritised the things that are most important, ask yourself, are the skills you have to make you productive more likely to be used best as an independent business person (such as a home-based person), or are they more suited to working in an existing business environment.

If you choose working in an existing business environment, always ensure you understand what your employer means by "being productive." These are not necessarily described in an employment contract.

CHAPTER 11

Managing Uncertainty

Stress can be described as the natural phenomenon of existence and it has been said: "Stress is like sand in an oyster. A little bit turns to a pearl but too much can kill the animal." The way we react to stress is different in everybody but one thing is for sure, if stress is not managed effectively it can be paralyzing and effect our health. For the period spent in career transition, there is a high level of stress associated with any adjustments. Equally for people in work, there are levels of stress which, if not tackled effectively, can lead to burnout.

The manage uncertainty chart shows the only thing that is constant is change and time. There is a push-pull effect between security and freedom which over a long period of time indicates our ability to handle uncertainty. It all comes back to knowing yourself so well that any change, be it small or large, is getting you closer to where you want to be in life.

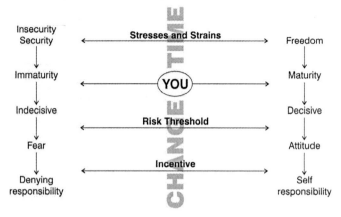

Manage Uncertainty Chart

Components of career transition that affects stress and time

Time analysis

Time is our best friend, but often we use it unwisely. The way we use our time is personal, however, those with a success consciousness tend to use their time wisely and manage it effectively. In times of transition there seems to be a lot more time, as things slow down and we learn more about the balance that is required in life.

We will now work out the way we use the 168 hours available to us in a week. Calculate the hours taken in each area of life listed in the last week. Total these up and graph them accordingly.

What is the most important area in your life, and are you giving this the time it deserves?

To manage uncertainty well, you need to know where your time is going now, then make changes so you spend time on what is important to you. Often, poor time manage-

Time Log — Hours Spent Each Day

	TOTAL	Mon	Tue	Wed	Thur	Fri	Sat	Sun
Sleep								
Relaxation								
Family Time								
Hygiene/Dress/Meals								
Travel								
Work								
Hobbies								
Committee Meetings								
Social								
Spiritual								
Housework								
Garden								
Watching TV, Video or DVD								
Other								
Hours Available	168	24	24	24	24	24	24	24

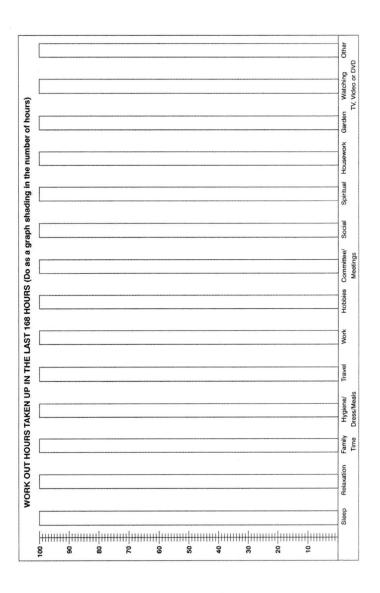

WORK OUT HOURS TAKEN UP IN THE LAST 168 HOURS (Do as a graph shading in the number of hours)

ment can be very stressful. At the end of a week, one's often saying: "If only I spent more time on a hobby or if only I spent more time with my family"

Five simple steps for time management:

1. Define your goals in a smart way.

> S = Specific
> M = Measurable
> A = Attainable
> R = Realistic
> T = Tangible or time driven

2. Create a simple table for each step in a series of activities to achieve a deadline. (a cinch by the inch, hard by the yard)

3. Do only one thing at a time. Plan every day's activities under categories like personal and business, etc.

4. Know how much your time is worth, e.g., $40 per hour.
   Simple calculation:
   Take number of hours you work per week
   Multiply no. of weeks in a year
   Subtract any holiday breaks
   Divide the year's hours into your annual income in the last 12 months.
   Ask yourself if everything you do is worth this rate of pay. Don't spend time on low-value things.

5. Know what is really essential in any project or goal. Put first things first. Can what has to be done be re-arranged and still achieve the same result, or can it be done by somebody else?

Some simple affirmations to endorse time management are:
• *I value my time.*
• *I grow and develop because of the importance of time.*
• *I am living a full and meaningful life: The present.*

Once you have a clear value of your time, you can understand whether the uncertainty is coming from internal or external sources.

CHAPTER 12

Opportunities Disguised in Change

A career transition brings change. When changing careers, there is often a period of transition. Change can come from two sources: Internal and / or external. The only one we can control is internal change. However, external change can bring about an internal response disguised in many ways, e.g., confusion and uncertainty. These experiences are transitions and form a crucial part of career development.

Change   ⟶   Transition   ⟶   Opportunity
(events or situations)   (experiences)   (dreams and goals)

The transition experience takes place on both individual and group levels and varies from person to person. However, regardless of the circumstances, it involves some resistance and passes through three overlapping phases.

1. An ending. We find it difficult to say goodbye to our old identity. Nevertheless, we must do so or let go of whatever is holding us back. This might be hard to do.

2. A neutral zone. This period can often be chaotic and a confusing time to the point where any thing seems possible, if only it would happen, which in turn adds to uncertainty. It is a time when one is stuck between two ways of doing and being, having lost the old and not yet found a new way, or solution that works. In short, there is nothing to hold on to. Other feelings we have are in "limbo," not able to move forward or being forced to wait.

3. A new beginning. We tend to resist trying something completely unfamiliar, but eventually we do feel normal again and accept the way new things are.

Then we see the past as a stepping stone to get to our new destination. For example, we may be seeking a career in network marketing and it is the second or third attempt. Then finally we succeed even though initial steps were unsatisfying or unsuccessful.

Three basic reasons people resist change are:

1. Fear. Everyone has a basic fear of the unknown that causes a natural resistance to change. Fear can be paralyzing if it is the dominant thought. Fear is strengthened by the possibility of failure. You may have given a token gesture to your own change accepting external influences, but resist with every fibre of your being any personality change. FEAR has been

described as an acronym for fantasised experiences (or false evidence) appearing real.

2. Indecision. You cannot suddenly change long-standing attitudes without by implication admitting you have been wrong, but accepting it seemed right at the time. It is important for your self-esteem and self-confidence to recognize that when developing a new attitude that you believe is right, you can feel at the same time that the old attitude wasn't necessarily wrong.

3. Lack of information. Some people don't change simply because they don't know where to begin. Many people have no idea of their goals, purpose or objectives in life.

So how can you start if you don't know where you are going?

Fear ⇄ Indecision ⇄ Lack of information

The reactions we have can affect the energy levels we have. Such things as confusion, fear, anger, and anxiety can lead to despair and depression at the extreme. We often feel the world doesn't understand us, nobody cares and we end up blaming or criticising others and resisting the change. This can lead to low energy levels. Low energy levels can lead to a R.U.T. A rut can be described as a grave without ends or rotten unforgettable times. Whichever way you look at it, they are often difficult to lift out of.

THE PAST   THE FUTURE

IN A RUT

The stages we go through from the past to accepting the future can be significant and do involve change. These are the same when in job transitions and include:

Denial (refusing to accept your current situation)
    ↓
Anger (blaming everybody else)
    ↓
Bargaining (looking for the easy way out)
    ↓
Despair (loss or absence of hope)
    ↓
Acceptance (taking self-responsibility)

This neutral zone in the transition process is a time of reorientation and renewal that makes a new beginning possible. If we manage to avoid this, we end up making false starts and postpone the real transition.

Shakespeare said:

"He/She that lacks time to mourn, lacks time to mend."

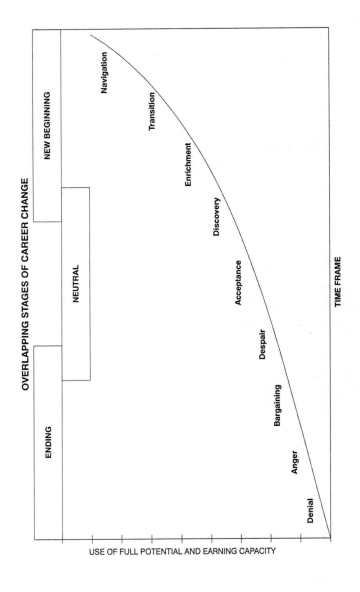

OVERLAPPING STAGES OF CAREER CHANGE

ENDING

NEUTRAL

NEW BEGINNING

Denial

Anger

Bargaining

Despair

Acceptance

Discovery

Enrichment

Transition

Navigation

USE OF FULL POTENTIAL AND EARNING CAPACITY

TIME FRAME

COACHING QUESTIONS:

1. What do you understand the relationship between transition and change to be?

2. Describe an experience where you have been through change in your life.

3. How do you relate this experience to transition?

4. Did the change or transition you went through affect your family?

5. What are your feelings about change?

6. Have you ever found yourself in the cycle of no energy and blaming others for the situation you are in?

After reviewing these questions, we suggest you choose one area in your life or career that you wish to change and take action now. Review the overlapping stages of career change and you will see how you move from the neutral zone to the new beginning.

In the process you go through discovery of self and potential for improving earning capacity. Often in this process the observation is made that change of a career may not be necessary, but simply to enrich an existing career, for example to take on a new role with an existing employer rather than a total career change. This is where the transition comes–in either progressing an existing career, or making a decision to build a new one. Navigation suggests moving in the direction you choose, but avoiding or overcoming obstacles that may be in your path. Navigating is also accepting that there may be no one ideal career, but rather a series or mixture of careers to achieve your maximum income potential. Often this is reflected in an entrepreneurial approach to career advancement.

Paul and Stephen saw opportunities disguised in change when they developed their business *Career Navigators* on the foundation of four stages: career discovery, career enrichment, career transition and then career navigation. Not only can each area be separate, but it is also possible to be in several stages at the same time, because they can express where you are in terms of career change. Once you have found the path to your new beginning, workforce security is enhanced.

CHAPTER 13

Workforce Security

Security is often related to safety. One of the greatest needs in life is feeling safe. Usually a lifestyle is linked to a career, and feelings of safety at work can be a measurement of success. When people believe they can get another career position easily, they feel safe and valued.

It is often perceived in society that to be secure, you need to be either in regular employment or a successful business owner / operator. Whereas security is simply a state of mind, for to be secure in oneself comes from a number of things. These include health, freedom, fruitful relationships and the like.

Unfortunately, workforce security can stifle growth, which leads to dissatisfaction. This in turn brings about feelings of loss and insecurity in life. Furthermore comes uncertainty with decision making, complacency, boredom and ultimately burnout.

Why do we rely on employment to be secure? Deep down we all need to feel needed and like to know we fit in. Employment has traditionally satisfied these human desires, so we can define this need as follows, using the acronym RELY:

Responsible - I am responsible and I like myself

Enthusiasm - I am happy / I enjoy being a team member

Loyalty - I am dedicated to myself / my employer

Yield - I am worthy and have a value for my life and time

How well you get on with other people is also a measurement of how secure you are in an environment. Stephen found this in his early career journey where he encountered people who did not like him or were jealous of his position. Many people have similar personal stories and feelings come up of "this is not what I thought it was," "as I am not getting on with the boss or a work colleague," or "what can I do now? I don't feel secure in my job."

To help define what security means and whether it could be an issue for you now or in the future, *read these questions and rate each on a scale of 1–8 (where 1 is not at all and 8 means you absolutely agree).*

☐ A. Does your present job or career(s) meet your future goals?

☐ B. Are you more secure this year compared to last year?

☐ C. Would you welcome independence as a result of losing your job?

☐ D. Do you think training at work will bring you job security?

☐ E. Do you welcome change at work?

☐ F. Do you feel in control of your own career?

☐ G. Do you appreciate and act on feedback from others concerning your career?

☐ H. Are you flexible when reversing decisions in the light of new evidence?

☐ I. Are you genuinely passionate about your career?

☐ J. How marketable do you consider yourself in the work-force?

☐ K. Do you believe your age is an advantage in your career?

☐ L. If you lost your job right now, would you get another one within a month?

☐ M. Do you have a supportive network around you for both your present job and any change?

☐ N. Do you see the need to change and move as a good thing in your job?

☐ O. Do you have a good relationship with your boss (or supervisor) and co-workers?

☐ P. Does your job or career(s) offer you personal growth?

☐ Q. Can you influence your employer's practices and policies?

☐ R. Do you have contingency plans in case of redundancy and illness?

☐ S. How well do you know your strengths and weaknesses and what you want out of life?

Add up your score = ☐

If your score was:-

19–38 You are not feeling secure in your present career nor are your plans clear.

39 -77 Change challenges you so career planning and control need to be addressed to achieve self-satisfaction. Your career is meeting most of your needs but you do not feel totally in control.

107-152 Your view on your present career is that it is meeting your needs and you are in control.

Do you still think you will have your present job:
(Tick the appropriate box)

☐ Next year ☐ 5 years from now ☐ 10 years from now

To what degree are you prepared to take risks to achieve your career objectives?
(Choose one by ticking the box which most applies to you at present)

☐ Not prepared to take a risk
☐ Will wait until something goes wrong
☐ Prepared to change work regularly to be fulfilled in my career

Now that the questionnaire has been completed, what have you learnt about the effect of security on your career?

- Consider the following concepts, so workplace or job security becomes less of an issue in the changing marketplace because one is destined to have several careers in a lifetime.

- Understand that security comes from within. If you plan in advance and set yourself a goal, you can control the direction of change. Take time out to reflect and keep balance in your life. To feel good about change, help create it.

- Learn to take responsibility for your own life and career. See your career as your individual course or progress in life through which you find meaning and purpose. It is a vehicle by which you support yourself and express yourself.

- Know and have a belief in yourself, for when you do, you create opportunities around you. Maintain good physical and emotional health. What good is wealth if you don't have your health?

- Have your income and identity in more than one work area. This can be seen in the dual nature of careers today and acts as a safety net. Successful people tend to do this in two ways. Some stay in employment while saving a nest egg until they have enough to take the risk of starting a business. Others build a business or income source part-time while retaining their primary employment. In this way they keep developing themselves, establish their market and it gives them something else to fall back on when things change.

- Find your own unique advantage in the marketplace.

- To increase your marketable skills, contribute your talents to where the company can best benefit from your skills, experience and expertise. You can then focus your energy on what needs doing.

- The organization of the future consists of a changing mix of projects. Career activities also fit into a project life cycle. *See chapter on career life cycle.*

- Be committed to continued learning and remember skills last only if there is a demand for them. However, most are transferable. So let self-renewal and self- learning become part of your philosophy.

- Network to find out where the growth and opportunities are in the future. These contacts can come through:
    1. People who work in other parts of your industry or field
    2. People who work in similar industries
    3. Participating in professional and trade associations
    4. A mentor or coach
    5. Other networking groups

- Future security will depend on developing three characteristics as a worker and a person according to William Bridges, the author of "Jobshift" (*Addison-Wesley Publishing Company 1994)*

    1. Employability: Comes from having the abilities and attitudes that make you an attractive prospect to employers.

    2. Being vendor-minded: Start thinking the employer is your customer rather than as an employee.

    3. Resiliency: The flexibility to adapt to change, to let go of the outdated, try the new, and accept disappointments as part of living with uncertainty.

Technology, customized production, re-engineering, downsizing, economic cycles and deregulation are changing the way organizations are run. New careers and job opportunities are emerging. More companies are reducing core staff and employing people on contract for specific projects. Numbers of self-employed are increasing, but it is not uncommon for some people to go back into the employed workforce after self-employment. This is probably because of the need for a different direction or the desire to be part of a team. Also, having transferable skills means, in the case of professional careers, opportunities are available globally. Some of the growth industries are likely to be leisure, tourism, health and education.

People are changing jobs more often, driving there own career development and end up frequently wanting to make a career change. It is also timely to consider another trend. The demographics of populations in many countries means we are likely to be working longer. The pressure to work means more career moves are likely to provide for longevity. Retirement and its funding as we know it today may no longer be applicable in the future.

What changes are occurring in your work environment?

As the world of work changes, security concerns increase, creating new patterns of opportunity. Constant change is forcing us to evaluate our jobs, careers, remuneration and lifestyle. For organizations and the people who staff and manage them, the only real security lies in the ability to grow, change and adapt.

CHAPTER 14

Sustaining Motivation

Whatever it is that drives you on a daily basis is critical to your success. Your motivation for action needs to be understood clearly. More important is the need to be able to sustain this for the achievement of career and life goals. Your personal goals are like the tip of an arrow. If they are not sharp (clearly defined), they cannot be easily achieved in a career.

As careers are normally undertaken in a business setting, it is important to understand how your personal goals and business goals fit together. Most businesses are structured around a vision. This is driven by a mission statement and supported by business goals. Employees help to achieve these. Staff are the key and therefore it is essential to achieve your personal goals through your work. Otherwise sustaining a high level of motivation is very difficult.

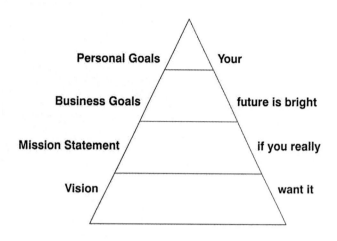

Personal goals are the pinnacle to the success of any business.

In the first place, all visions are the idea of an individual. This pioneer or leader usually gathers and develops the team to make this a reality. The passion developed is so great that whatever the hurdles, the motivation is sustained at all cost. The action taken as a result of this passion is usually moulded into a "mission statement" to reflect motivators necessary to achieve goals.

Mission statements are equally important to individuals so they can attract / create what they want in their lives. A simple personal mission statement could be,"I am happy, healthy and wealthy."

Business goals come out of making the mission statement happen. They are best set in association with management and individual team members. This in turn leads to career and personal achievements for all involved.

Personal goals are at the tip of the triangle (or arrowhead), because if you don't achieve personally in your career, it will not enable you to sustain motivation.

Your reasons for action

When you were a child your parent(s) and/or guardian(s) taught you right from wrong and how to care for yourself. The methods used varied and may have included praise for things well done, treats for following instructions and / or punishment when you did wrong.

Similarly, what motivates you now will fall into 3 main categories:

1. Attitudes—your thinking patterns. These can be positive and negative.

2. Incentive—What is in it for you.

3. Fear—Fantasized or past experiences that appear real in the present. (Or false evidence that appears real)

All three have a place, but interestingly motivation by fear or incentives alone tends to rely on external forces and they are not generally long-term motivators. Actions from your attitudes or the way you think are based on past conditioning. You have no control over this early conditioning. However, as you take personal responsibility in life, attitudes can be changed.

Everyone achieves, but you tend to be or become who you were conditioned to be. Therefore, if you desire to change your results, you need to change the ideas you are exposed to. If you seek to change your results, you must continue to expose yourself to new ideas. These ideas, when internalized, become habits of thinking which ultimately give rise to the automatic actions you take. So an old conditioned action is replaced by a new habit, e.g., lighting up a cigarette when stressed is replaced by 10 minutes brisk walking.

Most people will not change conditioned actions easily. In other words, you normally will not change your present habits (or go outside your present comfort zone) unless you find a habit that is more satisfying, e.g., a drink after work, watching TV or time management practices. Success means making a difference in whatever way is important to your life. Therefore, setting worthwhile goals is necessary for personal and business growth.

Maintaining momentum

To sustain motivation and achieve personal growth, you need to be exposed to ideas that move you towards the goals (results) that you desire. You need to know what results you want to achieve, so you can find ideas that match them. For example, for sales results you need activity, therefore accepting an activity report as appropriate is an essential element of success in sales.

Key ideas

- Change will bring discomfort. Don't be afraid of it. "Feel the fear and do it anyway."

- Expose yourself to ideas that will lead to positive habit patterns. We have a choice.

- Find out what motivates you.

Coaching questions:

1. Write down what motivates you to achieve personal goals. (Is *it fear, incentive or is it attitude?*)

2. Write down some of the actions you take automatically. (e.g., stopping and looking both ways before crossing the road.)

3. Who taught you these automatic actions?

4. What is one new habit you would like to develop in order to achieve your career goal? (e.g., to become a manager, it would be a good habit to read management magazines.)

Rediscover your passion

Once you understand your motivators and how to sustain motivation, the key is to ensure you have passion. This can be seen when the heart rules the head at all costs, or when you "pass I on" (share your experience with others). One way in which we show our passion is by following a pursuit relentlessly, regardless of reward. We can have a passion for many things, but it is normally to achieve, perform, succeed, have something better, be part of something, be somebody, be with somebody or to create something.

This is where it is wrong to stifle someone's passion. The reason or source of our passion can come through life lessons and / or hardships as well as challenges that encourage us to change or make better use of our talents and abilities. We all have a passion, but we don't all know what it is. Indeed it may even repeat the same message from time to time throughout life. It is often hidden, but when discovered will assist you to sustain motivation through life and your career(s).

Understand your values

At this point it is timely to mention values or beliefs, because we hold them dearly even though they may be hidden. When you know your passion, the values become easily recognized, because it is part of making that passion or dream or bigger picture happen. Don't be surprised if there is a close relationship between your values and passion. In fact, one helps you understand the other.

They can best be described as your lifestyle preferences and priorities. They reveal what will make you happy and what you really want. Your values give meaning or purpose to your life, are key motivators (make life worth living) and provide a way by which you measure your life. That is, they come from inside you. The most important values are your key long-term motivators, which are where real passion comes from.

Your passion and values are with you for life and from time to time they will be challenged as you pass through many life stages.

COACHING QUESTIONS:

1. What do you really stand for? If you are unsure, ask yourself what will you not stand for (or makes you unhappy), which gives a clue to the real you. Then you can select key words. These are your values.

2. What do you enjoy doing in life? *Knowing why will help you identify key values.*

3. Are there any other things you would like to achieve in life?

4. How would you like your life to be? *Consider your ideal career.*

CHAPTER 15

Your Ideal Career

We all have dreams of the ideal career. Often we spend part of our lives or a lifetime being who someone else (e.g., spouse, parent or sibling) wants us to be. The opportunities are only limited by your imagination and the desire to commit to a chosen career path.

You probably had many thoughts when you were young about what you wanted to do. However, you may have already spent part of your life following a path that was easy to fall into or that has been expected of you. This happens often in professional fields where a child is encouraged to follow in the footsteps of someone else. Some people have discovered their ideal careers through adversity or personal setback. Perhaps it is timely to ask what was the major influence that led to the job or career you are in right now.

During Paul's 30s, his father was diagnosed with breast cancer. Not knowing how long he would survive influenced him to make a career change. He transferred from one city to another to be close to family for support and miracu-

STEPHEN CONWAY & PAUL MEYER

lously he survived. Not until 6 years later was his father to be gainfully employed. This influenced Paul to pursue an ideal career that would give him independence, should a similar situation arise for him.

You cannot discover your ideal career by logic alone. There is an emotional side that lays buried in us that is often overlooked when seeking the best suited career. This will mean looking at your life in a holistic way. For example, some people say, "I see the good in everything I undertake and do." Such self-talk is a positive way of thinking. Others will say, "I am a goal achiever," and this is a way of being goal orientated towards success in life and a career. Finally, a self-motivated person will say to themselves and others, "I am responsible," because they accept that their present situation is in direct proportion to their actions and decisions of the past.

So are you prepared to grab the bull by the horns? If you are to follow your head and heart into that ideal career that you are passionate about, it will be like grabbing a bull by the horns. People may say, "You are mad," or, "Don't risk your health and safety," or even, "There is no money in that." You will need all the positive self-talk you can muster to get beyond what are basically other people's fears. Yes, there is an element of risk, but to realize your potential you will need to make changes and face all the obstacles and stumbling blocks head on.

Aspects of Your Life

A good start is to look at the different areas of life separately. The reason for this is it is far easier to have a career that fits your life than have a life that fits your career. The career and business aspects of life are normally the parts that become your income-earning vehicles. You may have heard the saying that "money is not everything," but it is definitely up there with oxygen. Which brings us to the physical and wellbeing aspect of life. It is critical to maintain your body in good working order.

You will find it equally important to maintain a healthy mind, which includes the spiritual and personal values part of life. The need to continue learning is often satisfied by ongoing education and hobbies. Life cannot all be hard work, so social and cultural activities need to be a part of a balanced lifestyle.

Family and home life are a critical link to success. It is important to maintain quality relationships throughout life. When you balance all of these areas and are happy moving towards your financial and investment goals, life runs more smoothly.

Your basic beliefs, ideas and experiences play an important role in determining your ideal career. Every aspect of your life needs to be considered when planning your future. To focus on the work aspect alone will cause stress in other areas of life. In time this will have a detrimental affect on your work or career. Usually this shows through as dissatisfaction, health problems and strained relationships.

The bright life is like the sun. When it shines brightly, we all feel warm and fuzzy. When it is not clear or partly clouded over, then life is not so bright. What is important is that we balance the activities in each area of life to maintain balance and stay in the right space. The career /business centre of life is often the axis or pivotal part of life. That means to be without it, we feel incomplete, lost or unable to be successful in life. Your career / business is like the filling in a hamburger bun. You could just eat the buns, but with a filling it is much more enjoyable.

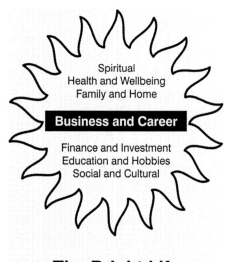

The Bright Life

To feel complete, we need to put energy into all aspects of life. In searching and choosing your career, you need to take stock of where you are now.

Where are you now in each area of life? Write three or four sentences under the following seven headings:

☐ 1. **Spiritual and Personal Values** For example, do you spend time alone with nature, meditate, attend a church, or give time or money to a charity?

☐ 2. **Health and Wellbeing** For example, do you have all the energy you want? Are you giving your body the food and exercise it deserves?

☐ 3. **Family and Home** For example, do you get the quality time you want with your family and/or is your home your palace? Do you have the loving relationship(s) you want?

☐ 4. **Career and Business** For example, are your talents and abilities being used in the right way to maximize your potential with the appropriate return?

☐ 5. **Financial and Investment** For example, are you happy with your net worth (what you own less what you owe) at this stage in your life and /or is your savings programme adequate for your future?

☐ 6. **Education and Hobbies** For example, are you adequately educated for your future ambitions? Do you have a hobby you feel passionate about that could be developed into an income?

☐ 7. **Social and Cultural** For example, how happy are you with the friends and social activities you engage in?

It is important to review how satisfied you are in each area of life. Give each area a rating of 1–5 where 1 = absolutely satisfied and 5 = totally dissatisfied. List in order of priority what changes you would like to make in each area of life. Start with the areas you are totally dissatisfied with first.

1. _____

2. _____

3. _____

4. _____

5. _____

6. _____

7. _____

You have now identified what order to commence working in each area of life right now.

Have you ever thought, if only I had my time over again? What would you like to have or be doing in your career right now that is not happening? If these prompters have your imagination running riot for that ideal career, then why is it not happening right now?

Be honest about these answers, because these may be the obstacles and /or hurdles that you have to overcome to move forward in your ideal career. If you have made these excuses before, you may be suffering from the "law of excutitus." This natural law of excuses is very infectious and can hold you back from your ideal career.

Longer term goals

Next, ask yourself, if everything goes perfectly in the next 3–5 years, what three things in each area of your life would you like to achieve? Setting goals enables you to focus on a direction for your life and career. People who set goals find a purpose and achieve more. That is because taking action based on these goals moves them towards what they want. There is then less waste of energy or time spent on activities that are not fulfilling.

Take whatever time is required and use your imagination, not allowing any fears or obstacles to restrict what you write down. If visualization does not work for you, ask the question what feels or sounds right for you in each area of life.

Have the life you want

THE THINGS I WILL HAVE ACCOMPLISHED IN
THE NEXT 3–5 YEARS ARE AS FOLLOWS:
(Write up to three things under each category)

Family & Home

Education & Hobbies

Social & Cultural

Health & Wellbeing

Financial & Investments

Spiritual & Values

Career & Business

Look at this regularly. Take some action each day on one of these areas. You will be amazed at the changes that come your way as a result of this exercise.

The same format can also be used on a yearly basis to develop strategies to achieve your 3–5 year longer term goals. Under the same headings, set your goals for each year. These goals can be flexible as changing circumstances permit each year.

Now study these longer term goals to ask what career is ideal to achieve these. For example, if a goal is to own a jet ski and you are a salesperson, would a career in jet ski sales move you towards your goal. Another example is if your goal is to have grandchildren and your offspring do not intend to have a family, would you consider involvement or ownership of an early childcare centre.

If this exercise does not bring about the ideal career to choose from, why not think about that dream career you may have had in your younger years, before all that influential conditioning. For example, many small boys dream of being a fireman and many girls dream of being a nurse, but in each of these careers there are many diversities and opportunities.

Face your excuses "head on" and set new goals to overcome them .Often the most difficult changes are the ones to become who we really are. Many people attempt to have more material possessions in order to be happy, but this often leaves feelings of unfulfillment, and usually results in them missing out in other areas of life.

Now describe your ideal career(s)

To use your potential, it is important to recognize that

there may be more than one career that suits your talents, skills, and experience.

The industry:

The size employer:

The position / role:

Paid employment or self-employment:

Remuneration and rewards:

Benefits of this ideal career:

Now go make it happen by following your dream and making "real" the ideal career that will assist you to realize all your personal goals. Good luck and don't forget there are many career choices on offer. Your ideal career should help you achieve your personal aspirations.

To assist with your career choice(s), below is a generic summary of the range of fields to consider. *(More extensive lists of fields of interest can be found through a variety of government, educational and community sources.)*

Question: Circle your field(s) of interest.

Administration–Clerical to managerial work

Agriculture–Farming and animals

Armed forces–Army, navy, air force

Arts - Performing, design arts and crafts, fine arts and crafts, literary arts,

Computing–Computer systems and design

Construction–Building, metal work, woodwork.

Distribution–Moving and storing materials

Education–Range from teaching early childhood to tertiary

Electronics–Construction, maintenance of equipment, telecommunications

Electrical work–Install and repair electrical equipment

Engineering–Electrical, mechanical, civil and chemical

Environment–Fishing, forestry, conservation.

Finance–Accounting, management, banking and insurance

Health–Naturopathy, nursing, medical

Horticulture–Plants, gardens and parks

Hospitality–Accommodation, food and beverage

Information–Library, media and technology

Law–Criminal, civil and legal matters

Manufacturing–Factory production

Office–Admin, customer services

Property–Real estate

Recreation–Community activity programmes

Research–Analysis of information

Sales and marketing–Advertising and public relations

Science–Life, physical, mathematical and social

Social work–Minister of religion, psychologist, human resources

Sport–All forms of exercise

Tourism–Hospitality and travel

In a changing world it is helpful to have more than one career option. Remember, there is more than one path to help you reach your ideal career.

CHAPTER 16

Work Choices

There are many work choices in the marketplace today. People have to choose and navigate the best way that will meet their needs. Many say that the traditional workplace is disappearing, so we are progressively being forced to look at different options. This is encouraging people to search out many opportunities that provide them with the lifestyle they prefer. Some examples of different work choices are briefly discussed under the following categories:

Employment contract workers

Job sharing

Community businesses

Working overseas

Co-operatives

Voluntary work

Self-employed

Employment contract workers

The introduction of individual contracts for both the short and long-term, salaried, waged and casual workers has become a trend in recent years. These contracts are often related to performance and the employer achieving measurable success levels. These forms of employment are often seen as shorter-term arrangements, whereas in years gone by it was most commonly part of a long-term career with one employer.

Job sharing

Increasingly we see the fit of work to suit people's lifestyles and domestic and personal commitments. A good example of this is where both partners are working in a relationship and one of the partners may need to job share to get adequate time to provide or develop relationships with offspring. Job sharing is a way of having dual people available for a particular position, with both parties working out the hours they need to achieve the assigned role. Job sharing can help many, including mature workers who are preparing for retirement, those wishing for flexible hours while studying and the disabled who want part-time work.

Community businesses

This form of business is often used when an area has had a downturn or perhaps as a result of a large community industry shutting down. It involves the combining of community resources, often in many different businesses, to achieve a given result. Not seen so prevalently, but this could well become a way of the future as unemployment becomes a challenge in areas where the population once grew from large business.

Working overseas

Often international experience is seen as an advantage for someone in their career. To work overseas or in another country for 2–3 years is seen as a strengthening and character-building opportunity. At times employers have not been keen to employ younger workers unless they have had some overseas experience or completed their renowned OE. This is because employers invest time and resources training younger staff, then find they leave and travel overseas before value is received for their investment. It is not unusual for workers in their 40's and 50's to seek out employment opportunities to widen their knowledge and gain valuable international business experience. With the global economy, more work is available in different countries as a result of skill shortages and changing population demographics.

Co-operatives

This type of work often involves sharing all resources to a given end. All parties may participate in full business activities, but not take on the total responsibility that would be engaged in independent self-employment. Examples of this arrangement are found in the pharmaceutical and automotive industries and it is common in the farming sector.

Voluntary work

Often this form of work is used for people to gain experience either within religious or non-profit organizations, which give unsupported financial assistance. For example Greenpeace or the Red Cross, where people work for no reward but gain experience and achieve a given result with something they are passionate about and committed to. Voluntary work is often undertaken during a career transition, where the discipline of work is maintained pending the next paid employment opportunity. What is important is that it enables one to add to their skill base, continue personal development, contribute and be part of their wider community. With the huge range of such work on offer, many careers have been restarted or new pathways found through this type of work.

Self-employed

Many people choose self-employment to achieve their lifestyle goals. The question of whether you are right for small business, is an issue that needs to be addressed at an early stage, before committing personal resources. Small business includes working from home, franchises, licensees and forms of direct marketing. Many people are driven to create a business in order to find a niche for themselves. Such reasons include being able to make their own decisions, a better lifestyle and to fulfill their own dreams or ambitions.

Some suggest small business once had a reputation for a high failure rate, but as the workforce structure is changing, the successes are growing as people are taking greater responsibility for planning, preparation and good advice.

Are you suited to small business?

This is a simple self-quiz for evaluating your own personality traits. Look at this list and you will see what the necessary traits are for starting a small business.

Under each question, tick the answer that reflects what you feel or comes closest to it. Be honest with yourself.

1. Are you self-motivated?

☐ a) I do things on my own. Nobody has to tell me what to do.

☐ b) Once someone gets me started, I keep going all right.

☐ c) Easy does it. I don't put myself out until I have to.

2. How do you feel about others?

☐ a) I like people, I can get along with just about anyone.

☐ b) I have lots of friends. I don't need anyone else.

☐ c) Most people annoy me.

3. Can you direct others?

☐ a) I can get just about everyone to go along when I start something.

☐ b) I can give the orders once told what we should do.

☐ c) I let someone else get things moving. Then I go along if I feel like it.

4. Can you take responsibility?

☐ a) I like to accept responsibility

☐ b) I'll take over if I have to, but rather let someone else be responsible.

☐ c) There's always other keen people around wanting to show how smart they are. I say let them.

5. How good an organizer are you?

☐ a) I like to have a plan before I start. I'm usually keen to get things started once a project is under way.

☐ b) I do alright unless things go wrong. Then I back out.

☐ c) You get all set and then something comes along and disrupts things. So I just take things as they come.

6. How good a worker are you?

☐ a) I keep going, as I am motivated. I don't mind working hard for something I want.

☐ b) I'll work hard until I've had enough.

☐ c) I can't see that hard work is worth it.

7. Can you make decisions?

☐ a) I can make up my mind quickly. It usually turns out okay, too.

☐ b) I can if I have plenty of time. If I have to make up my mind fast, I think maybe I should have decided the other way.

☐ c) I find it difficult to make decisions because of the fear I will not get it right.

8. Can people trust what you say?

☐ a) You bet they can. Yes, what I say I mean.

☐ b) I try to be honest all the time, but sometimes I just say what is easiest.

☐ c) So what if the other person doesn't know the difference.

9. Can you stick with it?

☐ a) If I make up my mind to do something, I don't let anything stop me.

☐ b) I usually finish what I start if there are no undue problems.

☐ c) If it doesn't go right I tend to switch off.

10. How good is your health?

☐ a) I can't remember the last time I was run down.

☐ b) I have enough energy for most things I want to do

☐ c) I run out of steam sooner than most of my friends seem to.

Please now count up the number of ticks and write in the space below.

Number of marks in A first box = _____

Number of marks in B second box = _____

Number of marks in C third box = _____

If you have a high number in the A category, you probably have what it takes to run a business.

If you have a high number in the B category, you are likely to have more challenges than you can possibly handle by yourself. Therefore it would be wise to find a partner who is strong in the points you are weak on.

If any marks are beside the C category, it could be difficult to find a good partner that would be able to replace this trait.

COACHING QUESTIONS:

1. Which of these seven work choices best fit into your ideal career right now?

2. Do you believe you are suited to self-employment? If not, have you identified an area you need to work on?

3. Is there another choice, other than selected in question 1, that also fits your talents and abilities?

One important thing when coming up with work options is to understand the benefits of goal-setting, particularly in relation to accepting responsibility for self-employment. However, these things apply to all achievements in life. The setting of clear and realistic goals gives the following benefits:

- Saves time

- Helps make good decisions

- Reduces conflict and enables thinking within values system

- Increases confidence

- Allows for improved use of resources

- Enables increased motivation of self and/or employees

- Gives greater control of results. Everything is measured in terms of output and results today.

- Gives improved communication. Once things are clearly specified it is easy to do.

In summary, whilst setting goals is important, it is necessary to affirm the ability to achieve goals and ensure that these are set in a measurable and realistic way. Stretch goals do require some managed discomfort. However, any personal growth gained will usually far outweigh the effort necessary to achieve the result desired. In other words, taking on a new challenge will lead to further success and increase your risk threshold. To assist with your work choice(s), the career direction analyzer can be useful to help you have a clearer focus.

Career Direction Analyser (CDA)

Using this analyser at regular intervals will bring in new ideas, increase awareness and open up opportunities for you.

A. Respond to each item below by circling the number that best describes you. In this analyser, if the statement is not like you at all circle number 1, or if it fits you perfectly circle number 5.

B. Then review your ratings and tick in the box applicable whether you are happy or unhappy.

		☺ ☹
1. I am positive about where my career is going	1 2 3 4 5	☐ ☐
2. I am self-motivated to achieve my goals	1 2 3 4 5	☐ ☐
3. I consciously look for opportunities around me	1 2 3 4 5	☐ ☐
4. I accept change easily	1 2 3 4 5	☐ ☐
5. I have purpose and meaning in my life	1 2 3 4 5	☐ ☐
6. I refuse to give up when obstacles come between me and my goals	1 2 3 4 5	☐ ☐
7. I am a team player	1 2 3 4 5	☐ ☐
8. I gain learning from others	1 2 3 4 5	☐ ☐
9. If it is to be, it's up to me	1 2 3 4 5	☐ ☐
10. I see problems disguised as opportunities	1 2 3 4 5	☐ ☐
11. I think more of the benefits I enjoy when I accomplish my goals than about the necessary sacrifices	1 2 3 4 5	☐ ☐
12. I am comfortable about accepting opportunities that come my way	1 2 3 4 5	☐ ☐

C. The areas you are unhappy with require action.

What have you learned from this exercise?

Have you identified a learning need for your future career direction?

CHAPTER 17

Career Life Cycle

The career life cycle is made up of a series of projects undertaken during the course of your life, and therefore it is necessary to define what a project is and how to manage one. Rory Burke, author of *Project Management Planning & Control Techniques, Burke Publishing 2003*, defined a project as a group of activities that have to be performed in a logical sequence to meet objectives outlined by the client. This could be likened to your career life cycle. These series of projects have certain features which include:

- A life cycle, e.g., career life cycle
- A start and finish date of a training course or on-the-job supervision
- A budget to pay your education or training
- A single point of responsibility. Only you can be responsible for your career.
- Involvement in teams or relationships, e.g., other staff, clients or mentors and coaches

In simple terms, the definition of project management

is making the project happen. In the case of careers, career management is simply making the career happen.

In viewing the life cycle model that follows, you will see that there are varying levels of effort required to achieve career goals. These start at an early age with our primary education. We then move through the teenage years, which challenge us to find our identity. Often there is a temporary period (usually in limbo, working or staying at school longer) before we accept that further tertiary education is necessary to achieve specific career objectives. During this time, many younger people may discover that they are not entirely suited to an academic pathway and instead may be more successful at a skill with their hands, such as taking up a trade.

In these early years, the cost to them and or their parent(s) is high in effort and financial resources (e.g., course fees, living away from home costs, etc.). Often, careers commence with a deficit net worth position, because students take out loans or have other commitments that are necessary to achieve a certain level of education.

As life is a journey, often in the early stages choosing a career does not come easily. The career life cycle may go through periods of transition, bringing indecision and the need to pursue various avenues to find the right career. Ultimately, your talents and abilities are best suited to a field or industry that your natural instincts tend towards. You will recognize that continued effort is necessary right throughout life to sustain career enrichment. By enrichment, we mean being fulfilled and effective in your life and career. This means that often people are faced with career change at various points in their life in response to the changing economies and technology.

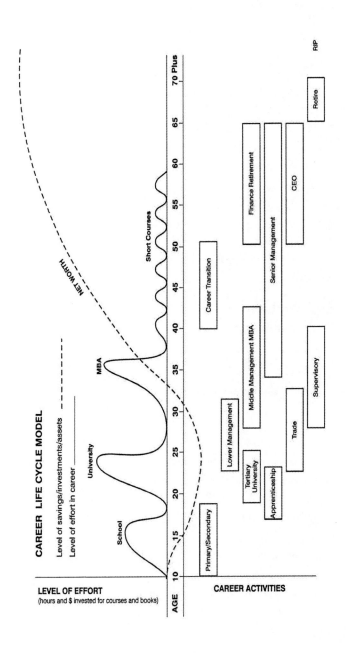

In our present day, it is not uncommon to see career changes more frequently, even during each decade. People now change jobs, or their roles can be redefined when a contract comes to an end. In some cases the average job or contract lasts only 1 or 2 years at a time. So change is here to stay in the near term. The responsibility stays with you, the individual, to ensure that you are putting in the effort. This may be a mid-life qualification or various short courses to maintain the growth necessary for varying work opportunities. You will have to be creative and use your life experience to decide how best to use your life potential. Most skills you have accumulated over life are capable of being transferable into a role in the workforce. The key is to retain your employability.

Now take the time to write what the ideal career will be to fulfill your life ambitions.

Refer to that chapter to help you. The career life cycle model is a creative tool to help you reflect where you have been, how you are doing and will enable you to project a future path for yourself.

You may have found that life does not always run smoothly. The same applies to careers. The career life cycle will show that there will be various stages in your career, whether this is jobs, employment, unemployment (transition), self-employment and /or businesses. All these stages have a beginning and an ending that form part of your career life cycle. It is critical that each stage be appropriately dealt with in order to move on in your career. All these stages involve some degree of exploration, getting established, increasing your financial worth, and making decisions to meet your changing needs.

By plotting your career life cycle, you will be able to relate the effort and time you have put into your career up to this present point. Your personal growth and earning capacity would normally increase in a shorter period of time as you make changes to subsequent careers. Let's now estimate your effort and net worth so you can recognize opportunities as they come along, or create them yourself. You should be able to see or feel your way along your path.

Exercise: On the chart.

- Mark the age you are now and go back and plot what effort (e.g., time, study, energy or enthusiasm) you have put into your career so far.

- Show how your net worth (the difference between what you own and what you owe) has been developed over the period of time to your present age.

- In the lower section, write in your career activities as they have taken place for you to date.

You now have a tool to show how your career is progressing. This includes evaluating whether you require further career enrichment. As you progress in your career, you will be able to plot your effort and net worth in relation to your career life cycle. It is also good for reflecting on your work/career path to date. In the next section you will see how your career bridge fits into a career life cycle.

CHAPTER 18

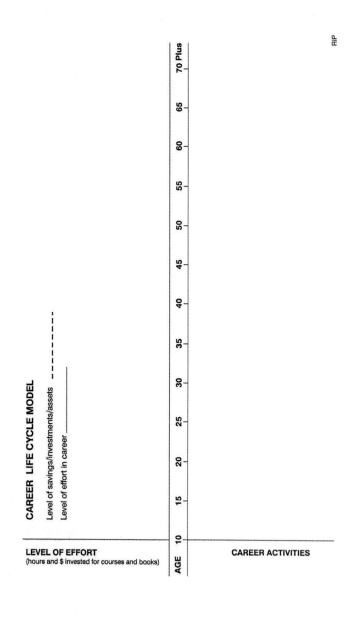

Your Career is Like a Bridge

Your career is like a bridge, because it needs to be planned with precision and detail, yet is flexible enough to be the pathway to your desires. By planning your career, you avoid leaving your success to luck alone. Luck is like "Leaving untimely chance to knock." With a career plan, you at least have a pathway to follow and measure your progress against. When you are in the right career, some talk about attracting luck. It is really a time when opportunity meets preparation. So leaving all success in your career to luck is unwise. Also, everyone's life is unique and luck shows up at different times for all of us. Not necessarily when we want it.

The career foundation

Your career foundation has two parts: where you are now and where you want to be. Similarly, a bridge spans between two points, and each needs a stable foundation. Where you are now is made up of your life experiences, training, past achievements, talents and abilities, and transferable skills.

Where you want to be is the career or work destination you chose to aim for. Between the two points you can either go down into a rut or you can build a bridge (career) to success. Either way, the choice is yours. The connection point is your pathway or journey through life, taking into account all the various aspects of life.

Building the bridge is hard work because it requires careful planning and management of resources to be progressive. Whereas slipping into a rut can be easier, but those rotten unforgettable times are often very draining on your resources and can even lead to despair.

Knowing yourself

Discovering your career is dependent on how well you know yourself. Now that you know where you are, you can use your vision, creativity, and innovation to develop your career plan. Do not be afraid to follow your intuition regarding career options. After all, ownership must rest with you. Remember the detail in planning a bridge and all the people involved. It helps to share the career journey with others. This includes friends, family, career specialists, or others who genuinely will encourage you to follow your career star. Confidence in achieving your desired career aspirations is demonstrated by actions you take. Life is not a trial run. Every day counts, so take action today. It has also been said in your journey, everything you do counts.

How long will it take you to build your career bridge? One day, one week, one month or one year. Some career plans start with a small step which leads on to the next. There is no right or wrong time frame, only that your plan should be developed in such a way that you allow sufficient flexibility to realise your full potential.

To know yourself well, there is a requirement to understand that life is full of transitional periods. For example, in a career the transition from paid employment to self-employment, corporate employment to small private enterprise, or customer services team member to manager of the customer services team. Before beginning to build your career bridge, undertake the "assessment transition threshold" exercise to understand your acceptance of change.

Assessing Transition Threshold

Write in the number that corresponds closest to your degree of agreement with each question, among the following options:

4 = totally happy
3 = happy
2 = happy sometimes
1 = not happy at all

☐ 1. I recognize the transition experience as an opportunity to be creative even though it can also be a difficult time.

☐ 2. I am aware that I have the resources to deal with the changes that are emerging in my life and career.

☐ 3. I believe that I have really come to terms with change in my career and can progress by taking little steps towards new goals.

☐ 4. I have created temporary support systems to help me through (between the old and new) the neutral zone.

☐ 5. I have someone with whom I can share my thoughts about my present situation or journey.

☐ 6. I have a personal stress and time management plan to handle uncertainty to make the transition experience more bearable.

☐ 7. I am aware of what I must change and let go of, especially in relation to self-image, expectations and assumptions about jobs.

☐ 8. I am using the transition period to rethink what it is I want to accomplish in my life for the future.

☐ 9. Specially, I am looking at who I really am today, what I really want out of my life, and what are my best talents and abilities.

☐ 10. I understand the transition period is preparing me to use more of my potential.

Based on your input in this personal transition survey, your individual score can be measured as follows:

32–40 You can accept change and be ready to move through transition positively.

22–30 You can accept change but have some reservations of how to cope with this in your present situation.

Under 20 You may not be accepting of change easily at the present time. It would be wise to ask yourself if there are some areas you would like to change, in order to improve your transition threshold.

Activity:
- To begin your own career bridge:
- Firstly, decide on what area of life you need to start. Often career planning begins with changes in other areas of life. *See chapter for your ideal career.*
- State the goal in the positive, e.g., "I am accomplishing…"
- Set deadlines and treat them like an air ticket. You will usually do anything to meet a plane trip.
- Your benefits must be personal and will help you to achieve your goals.
- The steps can be short-term (over a year) or take many years.
- A signature will be your commitment to yourself. Commitment may be defined as the determination, enthusiasm and energy you are prepared to put in. This career bridge forms part of your action plan for the future.

BUILDING YOUR CAREER BRIDGE IS LIKE WALKING UP A SET OF STEPS

Decide on area of life to begin:- ....

The goal is:- ....

The deadline is:- ....

The benefits are:-

a) _____

b) _____

c) _____

d) _____

e) _____

F) _____

Now commit to taking these steps

_____ _____
Signature   (Date Set)

5th step
I will take
/   /

4th step
I will take
/   /

3rd step
I will take
/   /

2nd step
I will take
/   /

1st step
I will take
/   /

The bridge can also be used as a "reflective tool" to retrace the steps to where you are now, and forms part of the career life cycle. For example: Where each prior step leads to the next one.

Step 1: The first step had been to secure employment in the industry and gain sufficient experience to make decisions to pursue a career in the chosen industry, banking.

Step 2: Next was a commitment to study a relevant degree qualification

Step 3: Senior banking experience to train for executive status.

Step 4: Several years of experience in the executive ranks in preparation for management.

Step 5: Manager at the peak of his/her career.

Remember to review your progress as often as you need to and adjust your steps or goals as circumstances permit. If you find yourself indecisive then there will be a need to review your decision-making process.

How to make a decision

In building your career bridge you will be faced with decisions. The following process applies to most business and work problems you will come across.

Consider the summary that follows to understand how to make good decisions and then apply this when using the career decision maker.

The steps are usually:

1. Define the problem

2. Collect information.

3. Consider the options.

4. Review findings of steps 1, 2 & 3. *(Sometimes it is appropriate to do this at different times if circumstances permit)*

5. Make a decision and take action.

Use problem solving before decision making, as the later depends on technical solutions available, and decision making is the best option which has the widest support.

The problem-solving process

Often we need to use the problem-solving process to identify what we need to make a decision on or about. Use the following points to ensure your process to identify a problem is fair and reasonable.

Attitudes are of primary importance, e.g., how do you think about the problem?

- Be aware that a problem does exist.
- Recognize what the problem actually is.
- Be objective, put your feelings aside.
- Set deadlines when solving problems.
- Regard problems as a challenge, not a burden.
- Visualise the problem you want to achieve by solving the problem.
- Solving problems requires knowledge.
- Be creative in finding solutions.
- Critical analysis of the solution is essential.

The decision making process

Use the following as a checklist of points to consider:

- Most decisions are small ones.
- All decisions involve a choice.
- Sound decisions are more related to common sense than intellect.

- The best decisions have a strong self-structure. (e.g., awareness and responsibility)
- Decisions are still made by people.
- Prepare for decision making adequately and appropriately.
- Accept only those decisions that are rightfully yours.
- Refuse to be pressurized.
- Know how important the decision is.
- Gather as much information as possible.
- Decide upon evidence, not inspiration.
- Implement decisions.
- Accept the risk of deciding.
- Always include an alternative.
- Match the decision with action.
- Follow-up.
- If the decision is wrong, don't be afraid to reverse it.
- Don't major on minors.
- Seek knowledge and informed advice.
- Success is built on relatively small victories.

Remember, the stronger our self-image, our self-confidence, and our determination to succeed, the better the success we will enjoy in problem solving and decision making.

The career decision maker incorporates steps and the process of decision making into a simple, practical form. It therefore is very useful for solving problems related to career matters or other areas of life. It can be used by those already in work or looking at other options. It is helpful when in

CAREER DECISION MAKER

What decision is needed?		Make decision by Date:
Internal	**Benefits of making this decision**	External

What information is needed?	Who do I need to talk to?
1	1
2	2
3	3
4	4
5	5
6	6
7	7
8	8

Look at the alternatives/options available	If I choose this alternative what outcome is likely. How will it affect my life?
1	
2	
3	
4	

What decision was made?	Date decision made

What results have been achieved?

career transition, as there could be obstacles that need a decision and action to overcome. As with any problem in life, a decision is needed and the pressure is often related to time. For example, a job offer may be received and it must be accepted or declined within a certain time frame. The career decision maker gives a simple outline for making the decision. Using this form on a regular basis can give a written record of how you arrived at making a decision. We use this process regularly in a work/employment situation, but often forget this is equally important to record in other areas of our life.

The important thing to remember is all decisions are based on information at a given time. Often there becomes a point where it is no longer practical to gather more information and a decision simply must be made. Ensure that decisions take into account the outcome for results of the action taken. Usually once an important decision is made, the relief of making a decision helps you to move forward.

The best decisions are made when you have considered the benefits *(not just financial),* looked at all the relevant information and shared with a trusted person the pros and the cons about the decision that is needed. The outcome can be both positive and negative, but most importantly is the effect this will have on your life overall.

Important decisions deserve reflection after the event, and often this can be summarized by asking what results have been achieved. The time you do this after a decision varies depending on the circumstances. Many decisions of the past reflect in the value you hold for yourself in the future.

CHAPTER 19

Valuing Your Career

Our career is generally the vehicle for providing income along with other satisfiers. So to value your career, you must know what your time is worth. That is how much you earn per hour, per day, per week and per year.

To calculate your hourly worth:

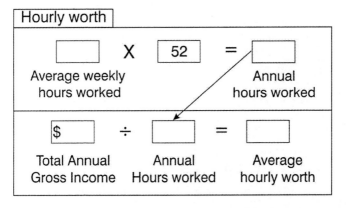

Are you happy with this? Would you like to decrease

the hours you work and increase your value? We should not look at work as just a job, but also as how to gain optimum value. This may be working on several businesses as a contract operator or perhaps as an owner. It may be developing a property portfolio and using the net sale of these properties as your income. The most common income is one mainstream career.

Often, we follow one career in our earlier work years so as to develop skills and the risk threshold to take on greater responsibilities. Usually these increased responsibilities bring greater income potential. As our thought pattern and confidence grows, so increases our value. Often new workforce people will work in a retail store for say $8.00 -$10.00 per hour, but later in life they would not work for less than say $40.00 per hour.

To help you put a value on yourself, take this opportunity to plot your own career value chart.

Looking in the example given:

Career A took 20 years to achieve $42,000 per annum income.

Career B, while going into deficit initially, moved up to over $60,000 per annum income in less than 10 years.

Career C over 10 years only had income of up to $10,000 per annum. This may have been purely from wages, or it could have been the income before tax of a small business.

The career on line D shows a declining income in the initial period, while developing perhaps a business venture, and then a sharp increase of value in a relatively short period of time.

Now value each period of your career separately. To complete your chart you will need to list the career categories you have worked in. It is also helpful to consider what you

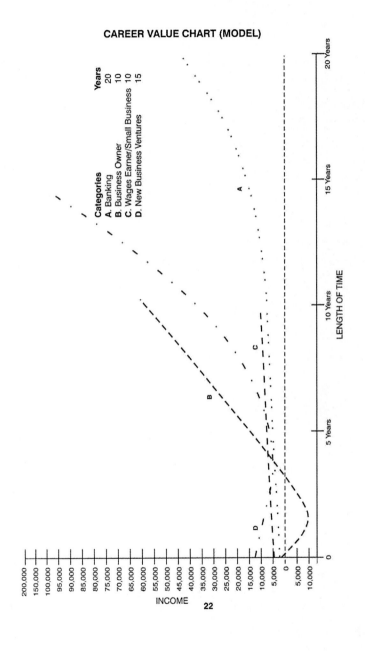

CAREER VALUE CHART (MODEL)

Categories	Years
A. Banking	20
B. Business Owner	10
C. Wages Earner/Small Business	10
D. New Business Ventures	15

LENGTH OF TIME

INCOME

22

147

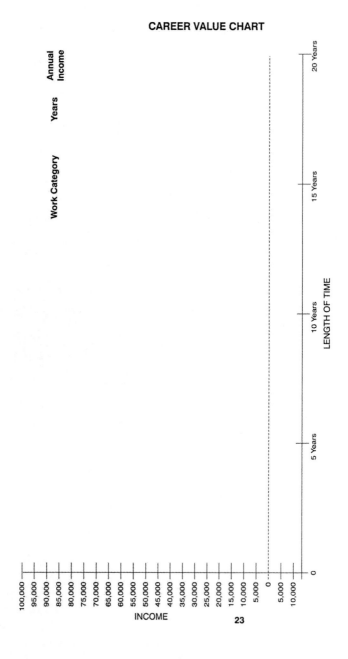

STEPHEN CONWAY & PAUL MEYER

148

foresee your next future move to be. So you could also plot a sample of how you would like that income to be.

Looking at the chart, you should be able to see that your career value has increased progressively as you made career changes, although occasionally this is not the case. Sometimes we may move into a career area that is not suitable and move out of this quite quickly with little if any financial returns. A major benefit of completing the career value chart is that you take a holistic view of your career/life span. When you make each career change it is normally best to see that the financial benefits come on stream as quickly as possible. Sometimes, as with a period of study before taking on a career move, there is a need for investment of time and resource before achieving financial career returns.

From this chart you will be able to identify which career change has given you the most value in the least period of time. Generally as you change careers, the income curve should grow more quickly, otherwise you may be minimizing your career value or choosing a strategic decline in career income.

Once you have completed your career value chart you are in a position to look at the reasons why you may not be satisfied with your present income level. If this is the case, we would suggest you look at the "career monitor identifier" (CMI), which starts with the statement which many people make–that their income is too low. Follow through this to look for areas you may need to address for change and to enhance your career value.

Now look at the CMI and you will see why you may have a lower income than you would like in terms of your true potential. We can attribute low income to many reasons, some of which are inappropriate employment, poor deci-

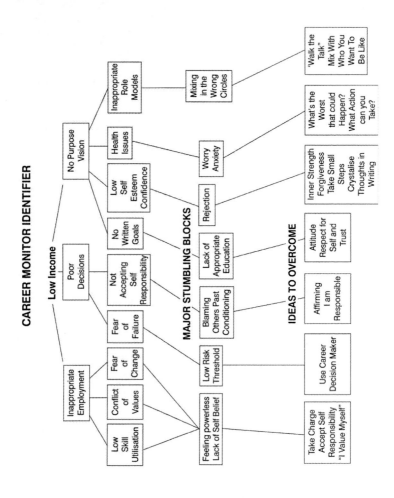

sions and / or no purpose or vision. Each of these causes, affect us in the way we view our life. Often people seen as late starters may well have symptoms which are caused by major stumbling blocks of which there are seven examples on the chart. Such things as low skill utilization, conflict of values, and fear of change normally stem from a feeling of powerlessness and lack of self-belief.

Career change is often driven by the need for increased income; however, there may be deeper reasons, such as a lack of training or direction, improved lifestyle aims, health factors or a need for a better balance in life. Once reasons are identified, the stumbling blocks, which can be either internal (need for personal growth) or external (e.g., economic conditions, debt, or things outside our direct influence), will require a new approach or fresh ideas to overcome them and to move forward. After reviewing the CMI, work through the following action to establish the best way to achieve your income goals.

Career Monitor Questionnaire

1. How much do you want to increase your income by:

per annum: _____

per week: _____

per hour: _____

2. List your major stumbling blocks:

3. Which stumbling blocks are holding you back the most?

4. If you overcome this stumbling block, will it increase your income? If you answer **yes,** go to question 5. If you answer **no,** then prioritise the stumbling block(s) to see which is the most important one to increase your income.

5. List things to overcome the stumbling block you have identified. Also a date when you wish to have this accomplished.

6. Write down some affirmations to help you achieve your new income goal. For example, "I am enjoying the reward of $ _____ per annum."

The ideas you need to expose yourself to will increase your knowledge and help overcome your stumbling block(s) and maximize your income potential. The self-talk you develop will empower you to follow your goals with passion and determination. Ideally, all career changes should lead to improved financial benefits; however, there are times when reduced financial benefits are appropriate, such as less working hours for improved wellbeing. Change can bring about the need to rebuild a career.

CHAPTER 20

Rebuild Your Career

Rebuilding your career is like "throwing a dart." We are all striving to hit the centre or highest value on the first throw, but really know it takes time to perfect.

Determination	(drive/ energy)
Attitude	(will / thinking)
Responsibility	(self)
Trust	(faith)

Determination can be gauged by your drive and energy to achieve a given project. For example people who find themselves shipwrecked and then floating in a life raft. They are determined to live even though the odds may be against them. Without a life threat, how determined are you? To rebuild a career takes much energy, and a determination not to surrender until your ultimate goal is achieved. This can take from months to years depending on one's circumstances.

STEPHEN CONWAY & PAUL MEYER

Attitude is simply the way you think about a matter. If you are in a flat where your flat mates are negative towards changing careers, you may need to find a life or career coach who can keep you focused. Attitude is shown also in our behaviours.

Today, behaviours that winners use to create successful careers are:

- They look after their mind and body with a focus on wellness.

- See relationships (personal and business) as critical to success.

- Have an unshakeable determination to achieve prede-termined (*planned*) personal and business goals.

- Have more than one way to approach a problem/chal-lenge.

- Learn from mistakes and are not afraid of setbacks.

- Gain something positive out of every event/experi-ence

- Have the ability to look ahead and act on that vision.

- Maintain a belief that things will work out no matter what ups and downs they encounter.

- Are willing to change and accept this change as the catalyst to all future success.

- Create something to look forward to and reward themselves for their achievements.

Successful people cope well in their careers when they behave and act like winners.

Responsibility comes back to the affirmation "I am responsible." When we accept change is best handled when we ourselves create it, then we can move forward fearlessly. The rebuilding of a career is a personal journey, and while many others can give a point of view or observation, the true responsibility is within each person.

Trust usually is extracted from our values and faith we have in our belief systems. The trust we put in ourselves can often be measured by the degree of trust we put in others. For example, in a harmonious relationship there needs to be mutual trust without conditions. In the work situation, employer and employee need unconditional trust that both will be fair and equitable. In today's society this is often formalized with an employment agreement or contract. You need to develop trust in rebuilding your career. That is, it involves faith and will take some time. Also, trust in yourself that after research and consultation with those who have experienced career rebuilding, that the way forward will be revealed. To really get to where you want to go in life, you need to throw the right dart at the right dart board *(your chosen career)*.

Rebuilding a career is often necessary at different life stages. At these times usually there is reflection of where you have come from in your career and where you would like to be. Life is often described in 7 year cycles. We hear of the "7 year itch" in relationships or the need to change careers. The following table gives the stages of life in 7-year periods. It is the work of Howard Small of New Zealand. Howard is a writer and teacher who is supportive of our work. We thank him for permission to use his life stages table taken from his book "Rainbows Of Success" *(Powerhouse Publications 1994)*.

LIFE STAGES

STAGE ONE Youth Growing Up	**Age 0 - 7** Rapid learning and growth	**Age 7 - 14** Acquiring knowledge and imitating adults	**Age 14 - 21** Search for identity
STAGE TWO Early Adulthood Trying to become somebody	**Age 21 - 28** Establishing yourself in the world	**Age 28 - 35** Acquiring assets, status and power	**Age 35 - 42** Searching for the meaning of life and lost youth
STAGE THREE Adulthood Knowing Yourself	**Age 42 - 49** The need to achieve one's ambition	**Age 49 - 56** Freedom of action and acquiring recognition	**Age 56 - 63** Looking for a new direction
STAGE FOUR Mature Adulthood Discovering what is important	**Age 63 - 70** Fulfilling lost dreams and appreciating life	**Age 70 - 77** Acquiring maturity and satisfaction	**Age 77 - 84** Searching for spiritual freedom
STAGE FIVE Senior Maturity Sharing wisdom	**Age 84 - 91** Memories	**Age 91 - 98** Enjoying life one day at a time	**Age 98 - 105+** Awaiting a call from your maker

No matter how secure you are in your career, these stages occur whether you are happy in your chosen career or not. How can you bank on where you are now in your career, providing what you want in the foreseeable future? No one banks on the present lasting forever. Once you have looked at your past, your conditioning and your potential, you are in a position to understand the drive you have, the attributes which make you a unique person, the talents and abilities that are within you and how your bank of achievements have created the worth that you are today.

When rebuilding your career there are four aspects of life which can help determine any fresh direction. They are drive, attributes, talents and achievements. Let's look at each in turn, followed with some brief questions to prompt you further.

Drive

Your driving force will guide you right through life. Drive is your inner passion, a definite purpose in life, what motivates you, what you most desire or what you would do if your life depended on it. If you cannot relate to this then the keys can be found in the sections on sustaining motivation and your ideal career earlier in this book.

To crystallize your thinking, write down three things you are passionate about.

1.

2.

3.

Another question you could ask is, if it were possible right now, what would you really want to do?

To show how your drive or desire has changed over the years complete the following statement:

I have gone from doing _____ work to wanting to do _____ work.

Through this process we are trying to activate the powerful motivation that is available to you, which is the theme of this book and a key to your career success. Knowing your drive will maintain your enthusiasm over a long period of time.

Attributes

These are your transferable skills and characteristics. There are a large number of transferable skills and one of the main strengths in today's marketplace is to be multi-skilled. Ideally we are looking at the things we do well or most enjoy, that are based around work or hobbies and other interests. Consider the following five main categories of transferable skills across a range of your different career options:

1. Imagination / matching skills

2. Interpersonal and communication skills

3. Data processing

4. Performance skills

5. Hands on skills

The list of skills is far more extensive than we can cover here, and is beyond the scope of this book. The purpose here is to "prompt ideas" about skills which can lead to type of industry and possible work roles as a signpost in your life journey.

In the following lists, place a tick by each of skills, under the five categories you can relate to / feel right and you most enjoy. The key here is to select the skills you already have which you like using. Add any others as appropriate.

Transferable skills general list:

1. Imagination / matching skills

Visual

____ Creating

____ Decorating

____ Designing

____ Layout

____ Shaping

____ *Other (specify)*_____

Projecting

____ Performing

____ Acting

____ Composing

____ Entertaining

____ Role-playing

____ *Other (specify)*_____

2. Interpersonal and communication skills

General

____ Interviewing

____ Instructing

____ Listening

____ Public speaking

____ Teaching/training

____ Telephone

____ Writing

____ *Other (specify)*_____

Relationship building

____ Caring

____ Counselling

____ Mentoring
____ Guiding/advising
____ Helping/supporting
____ Team Building
____ Coaching
____ *Other (specify)*_____

Problem solving

____ Negotiating
____ Problem solving
____ Resolving
____ Settling
____ *Other (specify)*_____

Marketing

____ Advertising
____ Marketing
____ Negotiating
____ Selling
____ Public relations
____ Prospecting
____ *Other (specify)*_____

3. Data processing

Thinking

____ Listening
____ Observing
____ Researching
____ *Other (specify)*_____

Language and ideas

____ Criticising
____ Defining
____ Editing

____ Interpreting
____ Preparing
____ Proofreading
____ Reporting
____ Revising
____ Summarising
____ *Other (specify)*_____

Facts and figures

____ Analyzing
____ Checking
____ Collating
____ Comparing
____ Compiling
____ Computing
____ Entering
____ Estimating
____ Filing
____ Graphing
____ Investigating
____ Measuring
____ Planning
____ Quoting
____ Recording
____ Tabulating
____ Testing
____ *Other (specify)*_____

4. Performance skills

Time

____ Meeting deadlines
____ Planning
____ Predicting

_____ Networking
_____ *Other (specify)*_____

Resources
_____ Allocating
_____ Arranging
_____ Budgeting
_____ Distributing
_____ Grouping
_____ Organising
_____ Sorting
_____ *Other (specify)*_____

People
_____ Co-ordinating
_____ Delegating
_____ Managing
_____ Supervising
_____ *Other (specify)*_____

5. Hands on skills
_____ Building
_____ Counting
_____ Creating
_____ Delivering
_____ Driving
_____ Fitting
_____ Fixing
_____ Installing
_____ Making
_____ Packing
_____ Processing
_____ Repairing
_____ Sorting

_____ Stacking
_____ *Other (specify)*_____

Source: Adapted from "The NZ Guide to transferable Skills"by Christine Dekker. *Random House NZ Publishers 1994*

COACHING QUESTIONS:

1. My key transferable skill(s) are:

2. From the remaining transferable skills you have not ticked, list the ones you now require, would like to learn, or need for your next career move.

Talents

The only real security is our talents and abilities. These are natural gifts, inborn qualities or fluency derived from practice or familiarity. As we go through various stages and challenges in life they may be discovered. Some are lucky because their talent is discovered or seen by others while they are young. Others have hidden talents which may surface later in life. What is important is the recognition that we are all different or unique in how we express ourselves in the world. Personal career profiling is very popular these days, but to find one that suits each person is a challenge. Often it is the simple or soft skills that are overlooked, that we need to acknowledge which have a bearing on our emotional fulfillment.

Examples of personal qualities that express your talents are:

adaptable	individualistic
analytical	intuitive
articulate	innovative
balanced	show integrity
calm	good listener
committed	loyal
conscientious	non-judgemental
courteous	open-minded
creative	patient
dedicated	punctual
determined	humble
discreet	reliable
empathetic	responsible
enthusiastic	resourceful
flexible	self-disciplined
free to choose	self-motivated
generous	thorough
honest	decisive

COACHING QUESTIONS:

1. Choose three key words from the list of personal qualities that express your talents and abilities. (e.g., I am calm under pressure.)

   1. _____

   2. _____

   3. _____

2. What do you consider your most unique talent, gift or skill in life to date?

3. What has a friend, coach or mentor said you have a talent for? *(We cannot always recognize our talents by looking inward, but others can see those abilities in us)*

Achievements

Everything you learn in life is an achievement. These include personal experiences, e.g., relationships and turning points, work and successes in other areas of life. This adds to our personal growth and fulfillment right through life. In fact, many gain a sense of purpose from their achievements. In terms of rebuilding your career, it is helpful to identify from your life journey what achievements or accomplishments are unique to yourself and can be used to your advantage. Use the "Life plan over the decades" sample and your CV to

STEPHEN CONWAY & PAUL MEYER

LIFE PLAN OVER THE DECADES

Your Life is like a Project
"Manage It"

INSTRUCTIONS

1 Put your year of birth at the bottom of column 1

2 In the steps 1 to 8 put years in 10 year steps, eg. year of birth 1952, step 1 1962, step 2 1972, etc. At your present age draw a line across the chart.

3 Complete each level as a summary of your achievements under the line, and expectations above the line, for each decade. (Include first 20 years as one summary because this is when your basic values, core conditioning, and upbringing establishes your foundation).

Column 1

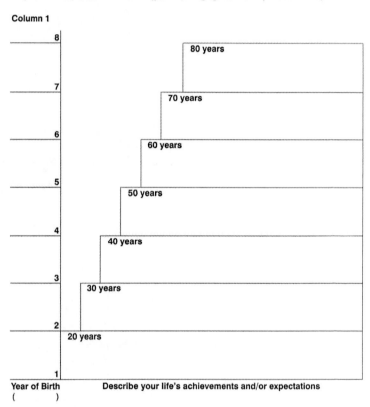

Year of Birth   Describe your life's achievements and/or expectations
(   )

166

help you remember key achievements and then answer the following questions:

COACHING QUESTIONS:

1. What are your three key achievements?

    1._____

    2._____

    3._____

2. Your expectations are an expansion of these successes and indicate the possibilities for your new work life. What are your expectations?

    1. In 2 years time _____

    2. In 3–5 years time *(refer to your ideal career)*

    _____

    3. In 10 years time _____

3. No look at life achievements would be complete without looking at the obstacles and difficulties you may have to address which influence your expectations. List the three key obstacles that prevent you from developing your talents or fulfilling your potential:

    1._____

    2._____

    3._____

The rebuilding of a career requires this careful analysis because it is the combination of achievements and the relevant experience gained that brings the confidence to forge ahead. Once crystallized, you are well prepared to market your talents and abilities with sincerity and genuineness. This degree of certainty helps you stay focused and rebuild the desired career with unswerving determination.

CHAPTER 21

Creative Career Marketing

Once you have used the tools in rebuilding your career, you are in a position to market your talents and abilities. Marketing yourself can be related to a business marketing plan. Our career marketing process is divided into eight quadrants.

As we discuss each quadrant you can check your progress under each section. Work through these in the order numbered on the octagon template. The first step is to *think* about your Career Marketing Plan (CMP) in such detail that you can decide on why this is important and how you will benefit from this effort. Now you are ready to *commit* to the activities necessary and by what time or deadline would you prefer to have these achieved by.

It is important to know your *present* situation to take stock of where you are now and list the appropriate information. The *vision* for your career will help establish a mission which as pursued will bring your CMP to life. Next

CREATIVE CAREER MARKETING

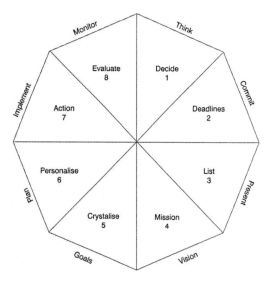

will be the detail of your *goals* for the *plan,* and stating these accurately and honestly will crystallize your expectations.

No surprises now, as you will need to *implement* the plan with determined and enthusiastic action to avoid any obstacles. The success of your CMP will be *monitored* as you evaluate your progress and record the milestones for continued motivation.

1. To think creatively one needs to empty their mind of all current clutter. This is often best achieved by freeing yourself of any distraction or influences that impact clear thinking. This can be achieved by immersing yourself in a place of serenity. For example using meditation or in a natural place such as by running water or with your favourite relaxing music. Now you are ready for clear thought about the best ways to market yourself for career

advancement. Your decision will be helped if you ask yourself the following questions:

A. Have I given sufficient thought to why I need to market myself? Y N

B. Do I understand the career decision making process? Y N

C. Am I aware of what my talents and abilities are? Y N

D. Have I given myself quality time to think clearly without interruption? Y N

E. Have I thought about what makes me happy? Y N

F. Now decide. Am I ready to market my talent and abilities? Y N

2. To commit honestly one must set a series of deadlines that lead to the desired result. In this case creative career marketing. Committing yourself is the next step after deciding because it incites action. It is important that you feel good about making your commitment, and once broken into mini steps with deadlines, it will make it appear achievable. It is often said anything worthwhile requires time and effort, so being committed to a career marketing strategy will take time, determination and patience for a successful outcome. Ask yourself the following questions to see if you are ready to commit now!

A. Am I prepared to commit time to marketing my talents and abilities? Y N

B. Do I have an adequate time management system in place? Y N

C. Do I use a planner daily either in written form or electronically? Y N

D. Am I prepared to market my talents and abilities despite the opposition I may encounter? Y N

E. Do I like myself unconditionally? Y N

F. Have I made an appointment with myself recently to advance my career? Y N

3. To acknowledge the present situation for your plan, list the information that will give all the base material for a strong foundation. As you gather these resources ask yourself these questions as a check list:

A. Have I made a written statement of where my talents and abilities are best suited right now?	Y N
B. Have I written a statement of where I am in my career progress right now?	Y N
C. Do I have a current CV /resume with a career objective?	Y N
D. Am I aware of what my transferable skills are?	Y N
E. Am I willing to change the risk and /or comfort zone thresholds I presently have?	Y N
F. Have I listed the things I am unhappy about with the present?	Y N

4. It has been said that without a vision we perish. So be it with a career. If we are completely at a loss as to what we envisage as the ideal career, then we will never discover it. In other words if we don't know where we are going, then all paths lead there! Reflect on the following to test if you have a vision.

A. Do I know where I want to be in 12 months?	Y N
Do I know where I want to be in 3/5 years?	Y N
Do I know where I want to be in 10 years?	Y N
B. Can I imagine a better future for myself?	Y N
C. Do I understand why I need a vision?	Y N
D. Have I a written vision?	Y N
E. Have I a mission statement that will see my vision realised?	Y N
F. Am I prepared to shift my paradigm to achieve my vision?	Y N

5. For many years Paul's' father would say, "You always need a project on." It wasn't until his mid 30's that Paul realized all he meant was always have a goal. It is not unusual in busy modern life, that those that have goals, clearly know where they are going. Adopt this approach with your CMP and the clear thought you develop from goal setting will reward you well. Use this check list to review your goals:

A. Do I have written goals for myself?   Y N

B. Do I have goals in all the major areas of my life written down?   Y N

C. Do I have written goals for a full year?   Y N

D. Do I believe goals need to be written down?   Y N

E. Have I set goals to make changes to myself?   Y N

F. Have I reviewed my personal goals this month?   Y N

6. All successful projects require a plan of which the detail varies according to its magnitude.With a CMP the importance and ownership is magnified through the process itself. As you look at various parts of your plan in detail it also helps to access what other support and resources you may need to carry it out. View these questions for prompts to ensure you have enough detail:

A. Is my plan personal to meet my own needs?   Y N

B. Is my plan to market my talents and abilities written down clearly?   Y N

C. Am I aware of how to create new opportunities to market myself?   Y N

D. Have I been honest with the obstacles to overcome to achieve my plan?   Y N

E. Has my plan taken into account global and economic trends?   Y N

F. Have I had my plan to market myself scrutinized by a career coach or independent professional.   Y N

7. Implementation is the way you take action. Without action there is no forward momentum. Making it happen is when the career marketing plan becomes a working tool to bring your vision to reality. Take time to view the questions and use them as a guide:

A. Have I diarised the deadlines for various steps in my plan?

B. Have I taken the following steps:

Listed all my network contacts, e.g., friends, business, clubs etc.	Y	N
Written _____ letters each week to prospects	Y	N
Phoned _____ prospects each day	Y	N
Visited _____ prospects to ask for advice	Y	N
Applied to _____ situations vacant each week	Y	N

C. Am I sufficiently prepared for job interviews with all relevant questions?   Y   N

D. Am I using new technology to market myself? (e.g.,email, fax, internet)   Y   N

E. Am I having fun implementing my plan?   Y   N

8. Self-actualization is important when empowering yourself to achieve your CMP. Monitor this by measurement of how you are progressing. Use the following to help monitor your achievement and develop tools that work for you.(e.g. the career progress tracker)

A. Have I set time weekly to review my progress?	Y	N
B. Do I keep appointments with myself?	Y	N
C. Have I had a follow-up meeting with my mentor?	Y	N
D. Have I used my career progress tracker this week? *(see example)*	Y	N
E. Have I used the job offer analyzer recently?	Y	N

This chapter has been about marketing yourself and after following the 8 steps, you will be in a position to know clearly where you are going. It will also be clear what it is you need to do. Use the career marketing plan outline to write in your own detail as it relates to you. Ensure you use the career progress tracker consistently, and if you are not receiving the job offers you would like, take time to analyse why. This will minimize the stress factors as you plan, do and review.

CAREER PROGRESS ACTION

CAREER PROGRESS TRACKER

	Persons Name & Phone No.	Company & Location	Date	Date Reply Received	Follow-Up	Progress & Comments
1						
2						
3						
4						
5						
6						
7						
8						
9						
10						
11						
12						
13						
14						
15						
16						

(S) Spoken　(M) Meeting　(P) Phone　(CV) Detail Sent　(E) Email

JOB OFFER ANALYSER

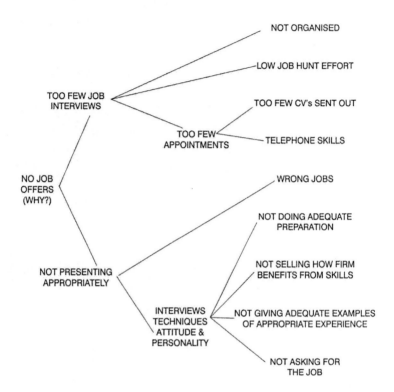

My Career Marketing Plan (CMP)

Think

I have made the following career decision

Commit

I commit to spending time to achieve the following deadlines

Present

My situation is as follows

Vision

I promise to

Goals

I have set the following goals by (include date)

Plan

My plan is to

Implement

I will take the following steps

Monitor

I will do these things to monitor the progress of my plan

CHAPTER 22

Minimize Career Stress

Stress is often associated with all the different stages of the career life cycle. This includes finding the right employer, meeting other people's expectations, the transition from job to job, changing careers and adjusting for retirement.

Paul's mother always told him, never be too busy not to stop and smell the flowers. Flowers are beauty and are the result of a seed sown, nurtured, watered, fertilised, and trimmed, and then they bloom with magnificent colour and grace. Flowers are also exposed to the elements, including sun, wind, rain, drought and other such weather conditions. If a flower is not watered, it causes stress and will wilt.

The human race has been subject to stress for as many years as we have historical records. This stress can be a strengthening factor or a weakening factor. As said earlier in the book, stress can also be likened to sand in an oyster. A little turns to a pearl but too much can kill the animal. Stress is defined as "a state of mental, emotional or other strain." (Compact Oxford English Dictionary *{Oxford University Press 2005})*

Many workplaces today are con-
cerned about safety of employees/
workers to the extent that many countries have laws that identify hazards to
avoid and/or minimize stress. It is now
commonly accepted as a health concern
in the workplace and often known as a
work hazard.

Sadly, stress can become a silent
killer if it is not managed effectively.
Often we do not learn from the early
signs that our body is giving us. In fact, stress is so persua-
sive, if you do not listen to the early signs, it has a way of
catching up on you. Just when you may think it has been
overcome or the signs have abated, it strikes with another
stunning blow. Paul remembers an experience in his life
where this led to panic attacks. At a time when his banking
career was progressing well, his wife and young family were
totally dependent on his continued income to service the
mortgage and meet the demands of life. Then, suddenly,
the unexpected news that his father had cancer—it was as if
the stress was too great. Not unusual, you may say, that's
happened to me or someone I know. Well, the reality is in
hindsight, Paul would have taken other steps to avoid the
unpleasantness of this stress.

So how do we minimize career stress? Firstly, we must
accept that stress is a normal part of life and work, and that
it is not a dirty word nor does it necessarily mean that you
are heading for mental instability. Let's look at stress as an
acronym.

S uccess
T ime
R esponses
E nergy
S ituation
S eparates

Often stress is associated with success. A saying once was that you promoted staff to their highest level of incompetency. If they coped with the increased responsibility they were ready for more. If they buckled under the strain, then that was as far as they would go.

Usually career stress falls into two main categories: that which accumulates over time or from one sudden event. For example, a sudden stressful situation would be trauma at work such as an armed robbery or witness to serious harm or death. A longer period of stress may result from a new promotion, where the initial impact is thrill, excitement, enthusiasm, then later to wane to repetitiveness, unreasonable changes or difficult customers, such as in debt collection.

As can be seen on the following chart, when comparing physical and mental career stress there are changing patterns throughout a career life cycle. In the early years we have more potential to cope with physical demands. However, as we progress through life our physical strength gives way to our mental strength. In other words, as we mature in life we become more mentally resilient, but physically we tend to become less active.

The commonly called "mid life crisis" between ages of 40–50 years is when equal amounts of physical and mental stress can be absorbed, but the body is beginning to show signs of not having the same long-term physical capacity.

Compare physical and mental career stress

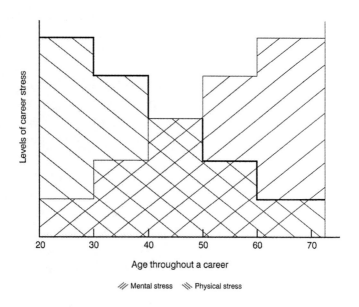

/// Mental stress   ** Physical stress

In early years the ability to cope physically is greater but as we age this capacity decreases, however there is a corresponding improvement in mental capacity to cope with greater career stress.

This is often when the mental capability increases and even when higher levels of responsibility are taken in careers.

Time is often perceived as a stressor. For example, you haven't got enough time to do what is required in a day, or some say time pushes you all the time. The way you react to time can cause stress. Ask yourself, why do you rush when you are running late? Is this a conditioned response? Paul was taught if you are not early you are late. As a consequence it has taken him many years not to worry or feel anxious when running late for a business appointment. Nowadays he just rings ahead or texts a message and the stress of running late is reduced.

Our response to situations often governs how the mind reacts. For example, if you were told there was a mouse in the corner of your office how would you respond?

While anxious moments for some, if compared to being told that a lion had just walked into the building, you are working in, how do you react now? The stress here is perceived by the thoughts of how a mouse or lion could hurt you.

Similarly, with stress in the workplace, it is often the different levels of responsibility that dictate the degree to which you are stressed. The experience and knowledge you have helps to cope with this stress. For example, many people in their early years, after completing their education to graduate level will travel outside their region or country to experience new opportunities. This can be a healthy way to test stress thresholds. Young enough to maintain good physical health and withstand the emotional strain that often comes with a new comfort zone. Stress saps energy and causes worry and anxiety. For this reason, the situation you choose for any career opportunity should be carefully considered.

In the work situation, we need to consider a number of contributors to stress. First is the environment. This is the physical place, its colours, ergonomics for operation of work, temperature and ventilation and so on. Then there is the people and their different personalities, the culture and chain of command, how people are treated and what methods of communication are used. In addition there is the location, the distance to travel, what forms of transport are available including appropriate parking. All of these factors contribute to the situation which, if not consistent with your preferred circumstances, can lead to career stress. For example, travel that involves long periods of isolation in heavy traffic can lead to stress. Working in an enclosed area with inappropriate lighting and/or ventilation can lead to stress and eventually distress or illness. Similarly just working alone for long periods can be stressful.

Your financial situation is also governed by the success of your career and earning capacity. Stress becomes a factor if income is not sufficient to provide for outgoings.

This is common even when you are doing work you are passionate about. Career stress builds up when income falls behind living expenses. To minimize the stress associated with financial challenges, a career should progressively improve income in line with the skills and abilities developed. Passion alone won't pay the bills.

The different situations that can separate types of career stress vary. At one end of the scale is unemployment and a desperate search for a job. At this point the inner stress is building up during the career search. It can become so overwhelming as to affect your reaction to the outer world. This then requires a degree of soul searching to gain the spiritual strength to accept the world is waiting for you.

The other end of the scale is the CEO who is so overwhelmed with the pressures of his/her role that the stress can influence their judgement. This often leads to poor life balance and a feeling that the firm must come first at all costs. This stress can become all consuming and there is the attitude to live to work rather than work to live.

The management of stress requires the separation of roles to see each in its true context. For example, if an employee is complaining to their supervisor irrationally, then the supervisor must separate that role from his/her inner-self. In other words, the employee is expressing concerns to the role of the supervisor, not the supervisor's personal feelings.

The best way to minimize career stress is to know yourself well. This includes the maintaining of a sense of humour and being able to detach from work influences.

Find other ways to deal with things that stress you out. For example, do something you like first, and then focus on something that is less enjoyable. Stephen has experienced that when he has a stressful work task it is best approached by changing the pattern or routine. So start with the thing you enjoy and the energy this generates helps to move on to a more stressful task. Alternatively, if you keep putting off a stressful task it builds up. So one way to cope with this is to do it first. The sense of relief brings satisfaction and the ability to move with activities that will build your confidence and self-esteem.

The Career Stress Test (CST)

Circle the answer that reflects your decision right now.

1. Is everyday a good day?   Yes / No

2. Do you have enough energy to get through the day?
        Yes / No

3. Do you feel successful and happy at work?   Yes /No

4. Are your personal values consistent with your
   work values?   Yes / No

5. Do you get on well with your work colleagues?   Yes / No

6. Are you being paid what you are worth?   Yes / No

7. Are you able to cope with your work load?   Yes / No

8. Does your work environment help you feel
relaxed?   Yes / No

9. Have you had fun at work this week?   Yes / No

10. Is your place of work engaging your best skills? Yes / No

11. Have you enough time to do the things you
are passionate about?   Yes / No

12. Do you have the flexibility in your present work
environment to fulfill your personal needs?   Yes / No

13. Is your income from career sources
adequate to meet your lifestyle expectations?   Yes / No

If you answered **Yes** to most of these questions, you are under minimal stress.

For those you indicated **No,** it is very important to take some steps to convert them to a yes. Use the following tools to help decide what you need to do.

Tools to minimize career stress

1. Understand yourself and know how you function in the workplace. For example, are you a person who is happy doing several things at once, but not finishing any, or the person who likes to do one thing at a time to completion. Being in the wrong role creates career stress.

2. Accept from the start there is a certain amount of stress in the workplace. Take this as a challenge and then as you become more familiar with the role, it becomes less stressful.

3. Use effective time management systems. Many claim the to-do list is the best way to prioritise activities. Paul once learned that to-do lists are stress lists. So he now uses the term "areas of responsibility"–for example home, staff, premises–and writing under each develops the priorities he has to undertake.

4. Use affirmations on a daily basis to reinforce attitudes required. For example, "I enjoy a stress-free environment." This self-talk helps prepare you better for a stressful situation.

5. Detach from your work activities at the appropriate breaks. Some enjoy reading in their lunch time, others go for a run.

6. Visualise at times when a new perspective is needed. Paul enjoys focusing on a calm beach scene to obtain an inner peace which he can then apply to the present situation. Also using spiritual tools like meditation, either alone or as part of a group where you are accepted for who you really are, helps reduce stress.

7. Have a laugh. Use a sense of humour to lighten the situation. Often this contributes to a more relaxed environment and reduces tension. Take time out to listen or tell a joke to rest the mind. See earlier section in this book *It's fun to work.*

8. Talk to someone. Often people are relieved of an anxious situation by talking to someone. Usually a trusted colleague, friend or family member will need to listen. If this

is not possible one of the support agencies may be able to help.

9. Cut back on the hours of work. Often people work on at all costs to themselves or those they love. Money alone will not motivate long term. So often saying no is the only way to reduce stress.

10. Have outside interests so the mind is not always on the job. Select hobbies that will invigorate and refresh and do exercise, the benefit of which clears the mind.

11. If you are under a lot of stress at work, meditation / prayer or a higher belief system that things will get better, will help you cope.

12. Review dietary intake to ensure it is supporting your desired lifestyle.

13. Seek out professional opinion on areas to support your wellbeing.

14. Review budget and present spending patterns. Renegotiate remuneration and if necessary consider higher paid employment. Alternatively, a secondary source of income might reduce the stress of financial pressure.

The joy of the journey "stress free" is about working happily. Choose a career that you are passionate about that helps you feel as though you are getting to where you want to go. Understanding that stress is a natural part of achievement minimizes the effects of unhealthy stress. If you find you are not in control of your time, you need to take firm action to minimize the interruptions to your priority activities. An example would be not to allow a mobile phone to govern your time but to schedule a specific time to clear messages and return calls.

Minimizing career stress includes a healthy exercise regime and feeding the body and mind with appropriate ingredients. A healthy, stress-free person will approach the longest holiday of their life, retirement, with positive expectation. Whether we like it or not, our life spans are extending dramatically. Take care and look after yourself sensibly to minimize stress.

COACHING QUESTIONS:

1. List what is causing you stress at the moment.

2. What do you see as the benefits of career stress to you? (Example: increasing comfort zone, promotion, able to be faster, cope with more.)

3. Take time to list some disadvantages of career stress. (Example: how does it affect finances, health and other areas of life.)

4. Select tools that will help reduce career stress.

CHAPTER 23

The Longest Holiday of Your Life

Retirement Trends

The concept of retirement appears to have evolved from the tradition of moving from long-term employment at a certain age to those leisure years where there is freedom and independence. This independence was often perceived as freedom of time, a safe place to live, continued income in some form of superannuation (private and /or state), and health and wellbeing to follow dream pursuits, particularly if they hadn't been done earlier in life.

The need to retire at a certain stage comes from the foundation of rigid careers that offered security and demanded loyalty and long-term service to be successful. Nowadays careers are far more transient, and often a number of different careers are experienced in a lifetime. Increasingly, we have a wider range of choices available to us and we generally stay in jobs for shorter times with each employer or seek out other ways to express our talents.

As with a career plan, so is the need to plan for the longest holiday of your life or that point in time when the regular money flow from paid work activities, stops. Reaching this point in life is yet another transition that, if not prepared for adequately, can be extremely stressful.

When we are young and so busy establishing an identity, securing relationships and building careers, retirement is considered far off and not given attention. In the mid years we are just so busy with the commitments we have created that we leave things to later. Next we realize the age of retirement is looming and the concern becomes, how do we cope with this fast approaching end to our working life? Most are seeking to secure lifestyle freedom safely at this time in life.

The website www.moneycentral.msn.com/retire/home.asp has a forward-looking "life expectancy calculator." Life expectancy from age 90 upwards is now not uncommon. While research reveals our populations are living longer, in many cases much longer, the time of retirement is no fun without good health and sufficient wealth to survive. We have given this time in life a new term: *Holtirement.* Not only do we "holt" from working, but we also need health, opportunity, leisure and time in our retirement. In the future retirement could be further out and many may actually be able to enjoy a new form of personal and/or spiritual development at this mature stage, particularly as society adjusts to new ways of working and living.

Working patterns at Holtirement

Life can be considered in 3 age blocks:

0	21	66	RIP
Educational Years	Earning Years	Holtirement Years	

The success of holtirement years is dependent on good education and wise creation of wealth during earning years. This often requires input from many sources during a lifetime.

Do working patterns affect holtirement? Most definitely and many employees move from full employment to part-time hours leading to the necessary adjustments both socially and financially. It is a good idea to plan what changes will be necessary for any budget variables. In fact, a year before holtirement is a good time to test the new budget. Can you live on the changed financial circumstances?

While career potential is often perceived at a maximum at the time of holtirement, in fact many revert to contractual work on an hourly rate, greater than in their last role. For example, a senior executive may be earning 250,000 per annum at holtirement for 50 working hours per week. In holtirement they decide to contract their management services at 125.00 per hour for 20 hours per week and produce 130,000 for these reduced hours. In fact, their hourly value has gone up 30% (from 98.15 to 125.00), but of course they have different overheads. This is one new working pattern that complements this new holtirement. Some people who retire probably may have an income base which allows them to do voluntary work. This helps keep a good social sphere of friends and is like a continuation of a career they enjoy without the pressures of an employer.

Social aspects

Social adjustment after paid work usually requires a concentrated effort well before holtirement. It is necessary to review your social network on the basis of who will survive the time you leave or change your career. Often people are very lonely during the longest holiday of their life if all their social sphere is left behind when leaving a place of work.

The building of friends and social acquaintances who can be supportive and those who you have regular contact with develops over time and needs to be a deliberate activity leading up to holtirement. In this regard, the maintenance of family relationships will become more important as greater time is available at these maturing years. For example, to speak with someone in holtirement, often their whole world revolves around their grandchildren.

Looking at the plan

For the most rewarding holtirement and to fully enjoy this period of health, opportunity, leisure and time, it is advantageous to plan for its success as you would plan for a career. In other words, plan for a career in holtirement. The plan can be likened to the plan to build a bridge. A bridge is built from one point to another and is the vision of a person to span a space, whereas the holtirement plan is to span a space of time. Your plan should be developed in such a way to have enough detail to make the structure solid, but flexible enough to make the bridge adjustable for changing circumstances along the way. For example, if a serious health ailment was to change your life expectancy, then your holtirement plan would need to be adjusted to meet this changed situation. A form of risk insurance which became payable at such a point of serious illness would be a way to plan for such a contingency leading to holtirement.

Your Holtirement Career Plan

This should include the following headings to give peace of mind throughout your changing careers. Under each of the headings are some questions to help you draft the outline for your holtirement career plan.

Estimation of longevity

1. What age did your grandparents live to?

2. How does this compare to your parents age?

3. What is your own life expectancy?

4. How is your health, based on lifestyle and present habits?

5. What is the current life expectancy in your country?

Maintenance of health and wellbeing

1. How are you going to maintain health to live longer?

2. What life changes are affecting your health now?

3. What improvement would you like to make to your health?

4. Have you considered all alternatives for any medical conditions?

5. Is your fitness and weight conducive with wellbeing?

6. What physical activity could you do?

Anticipated environment and surroundings

1. Where would you like to retire?

2. What surroundings will you want in retirement?

3. Are there service providers you will require nearby in holtirement?

4. What family considerations do you have to make?

A place or accommodation needs

1. Do you wish to be in your own home?

2. Is your house suitable if you become less mobile?

3. Have you considered retirement homes?

Financial and lifestyle expectations

1. Do you know how much you need to retire?

2. Have you an income in holtirement?

3. What lifestyle assets will you need?

4. Is adequate resource available for health needs and emergencies?

Social and friendship ideals

1. How many friends would you like in holtirement?

2. What could you do to have a balanced social structure outside work?

3. What interests / hobbies do you have that include friendships?

Leisure, travel and pursuits

1. What are your travel ambitions?

2. Have you allowed for holidays each year?

3. What hobbies would you like to pursue?

Learning

1. Is there any further personal and/or career development you could do?

2. What forms of relaxation and self-awareness would be helpful for your spiritual wellbeing?

Work

1. Is there any voluntary work that would enable you to contribute to your community? (e.g., teaching, mentoring)

2. What forms of paid work are available to you? (This could be on a part-time or temporary contract basis.)

Legal aspects

1. Are family assets suitably protected?

2. Have you considered wills and/or powers of attorney?

3. What arrangements do you have, if you become unable to manage your affairs?

4. Are assets suitably insured?

Other areas

1. Have you spread your financial risks?

2. What else would you like to do in your life journey, but have put off to date that gives you satisfaction and a sense of fulfillment?

Now you can draw up your holtirement plan using these headings as a guide and adding any others you consider necessary. This acts like a goal-setter to take you in the direction you want to go. You can now take a look at the journey of life and see how careers have formed and brought you to where you are today. In fact, your life is a reflection of your career and life journey influenced by your choices. The next chapter will link this to your complete career journey.

CHAPTER 24

Your Career Journey

All journeys start with a beginning, but often we do not know the destination when we start. It has been said that if you don't know where you are going, then all roads you will take lead there. This book started with playing hide and seek. In this game you hide but know you will eventually be safely found. In careers we can hide behind the comfort of many things, such as job security. At that point your potential may not be fully recognized.

When you played hide and seek as a child you knew the person who was seeking you out. Career potential can be suppressed or stifled through other influences. Who is seeking you out? Is it something greater than you? Is it the spiritual awareness to bring you faith and strength, sufficient to pursue the passion of your dreams? Or is there an unanswered question that there is something else. Please don't hide any longer after reading this book or wait for a miracle. It is within you to take the steps to have the career journey you deserve. No one will seek this out for you. It is your own responsibility.

A career journey can take you down many paths. It can be a long and winding road, climbing a hill (where the view is much clearer), or travelling through a dark tunnel where it takes time to come out the other side and see the light again. Career journeys can have any of these experiences. These are best managed if you understand that life is an inner journey that urges you to change regularly, repeating itself on the way to reinforce the spiritual destiny that you are deserving of. So a career journey includes physical, financial, mental, emotional and spiritual aspects. This book has been about seeing the complete picture for your life so that you can adapt to and flow with change.

We have an emotional connection with our work which is often tested during the hard times. During such times we develop character to cope with the twists and turns of life. It is through our emotions that we experience a deeper understanding of who we are, what we would like and where we could be. Indeed, one seems to experience many obstacles, even rejection, setbacks or failure, before entering into a more positive future. Life is not always what it appears to be. There is a reason for everything and everything has a reason. We are all unique and have something to offer or contribute to the world. No one else in the world is like you.

If you are lost or lacking direction
The answer is within you
As your life unfolds the solution will be revealed
Then you will see you are unique
That is your gift
Let your light shine

All great things start with small beginnings. So it is with careers. As you come through the career journey of discovery, enrichment, and transition, you come to a point of navigation which can be "plain sailing" in the career journey.

All your wealth of experience and knowledge combined will allow you to take control of your future. This can be

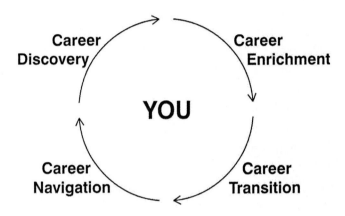

described as career navigation. From this point on you can use more of your potential, given that navigation revolves around following your life and career map as you develop independence. This independence strengthens self-esteem and brings a realisation that your life is far more than you ever imagined.

All this culminates in the understanding of the changing workplace, in which careers, jobs and work are all going through a permanent transformation. You may be surprised to learn the people helping you navigate through your career journey can include your family, friends, and offspring, who are all wishing to share in your journey of success.

As you progress through your career journey, you may

find that navigation is not necessarily the end of your career experience. Often we have to revisit our career discovery area to ensure that future navigation of our career does fit within our core individual values and lifetime goals.

The stages of career discovery, career enrichment, career transition and career navigation were born out of the author's development of a series of modules to help clients through these steps in their careers. This has been a journey, which has evolved over a long period of time as patience and persistence needed to be exercised. Eight years later it became the foundation material for this book, just like light at the end of the tunnel.

The following chart illustrates the *career challenge cycle.* The cycle is related to a 12-hour clock. Time varies in each career stage and this involves the need for action, to plan and make change. At 12 o'clock, the career is satisfying and achieving goals. At some point a "rut" or event leads to unhappiness, and this sets off the cycle to obtain information for new decisions. Once a decision is confidently made, the planning can begin. As you pass 6 o'clock, you identify the skills and talents needed to make any change. Then, between 9 and 12 o'clock, you reach a level where rewards are gained for the choices and the effort during the rest of the cycle.

The career journey is about self-discovery and understanding that one's personal fulfillment is paramount to any successful career. Once personal objectives and goals are crystal clear, then a decision can be made whether to enrich a present career or move on to a new one. Either outcome would lead to transition. That is transition to another career or transition to new responsibilities within a current work environment. After this stage, comes planning for change

Career Challenge Cycle

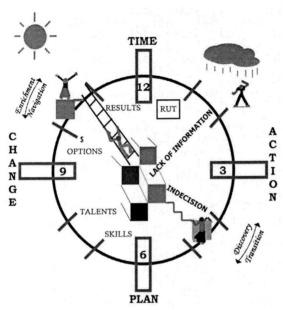

and considering options for the navigation of a chosen career.

To take an analogy, think about your career like a lone yachtsperson thinks about sailing around the world. First of all they have the passion or desire to discover the world. They then have the ability to stand back and look at the total challenge so they know what things require planning and action to achieve the objective. Then comes the transition, which is looking at what is needed to get through the changing weathers and storms that may be on the world's huge oceans. Finally we come to navigating the journey, and this journey includes learning from the experiences through discovery, enrichment, transition and taking control of your life (the yacht), which is now built to take you where you want to go. Ensure your career is taking you in the right direction.

It is the same with careers as it is to the lone yachtsperson. You need a vision and passion with the ability to stand back and look at the bigger picture, and then choose the vehicle that is going to be able to weather the storms to achieve the given objectives you have within your career ambitions. However, if only the first 3 ingredients are in place and we do not navigate the journey, it would be like a yacht without a rudder unable to be steered.

Similarly, with success in careers, if one believes they can start at a high level of responsibility without appropriate preparation and training, then often there is disappointment. As it is said that the only job / career where you start at the top is digging a hole.

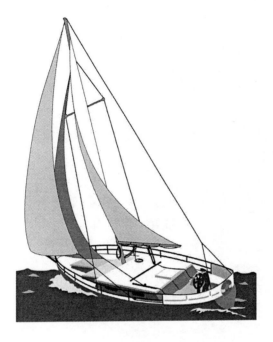

Behave like a winner

The body achieves what the mind believes. Winners achieve what their dominant behaviour and actions portray. Now take a few moments to see if your behaviour is consistent with your goals and career journey.

Complete the following to see what your dominant success characteristics are:

1. Underline the word(s) on the left or right that best describes you at present. Be honest with yourself as this is for your own self-evaluation.

2. Now put a tick or cross in the section provided whether you are happy or unhappy with the descriptions you have underlined.

✓	X	
		Realistic
		Value time
		Accepting total responsibility
		Disciplined
		Good self-esteem
		Always looking for ideas
		Proactive
		Good attitude (I can)
		Inspired
		Corrects wrong actions
		Around people who support you
		Good reader, listener, observer
		Has goals and plan
		Saves money
		Lives today
		Does homework
		Focuses on others
		Has options
		Compliments others
		Majors on major things
		Does it right
		Student of consequences
		Persistent
		Welcome change
		Has humility
		Takes good care of resources
		Giver
		Law Keeper
		Open minded
		Organised
		Tries to simplify
		Good vocabulary

✓	X	
		False expectations
		No value on time
		Blame others or circumstances
		No discipline
		No self-esteem
		Quit looking for ideas
		Reactive
		Poor attitude (I can't)
		Not inspired
		Continues wrong actions
		No people to support you
		Poor reader, listener, observer
		No goals and plan
		Spends money
		Lives in past or future
		No extra effort
		Self focus
		No options
		Complains
		Majors on minors
		Takes shortcuts
		Ignores consequences
		Gives up
		Do not like change
		Has pride
		Mishandles resources
		Taker
		Law breaker
		Prejudice
		Disorganised
		Tries to complicate
		Poor Vocabulary

Behaviour matched with goals to succeed in a career ensures that the career journey is both fulfilling and rewarding.

Back in the introduction to this book, we posed the question, do you have a career for life? By now, you can see hidden within the career stages and life cycle is the message that your career is your life and later on is the revelation that your life has been your career, whatever form that takes.

As we set out on our journey to write this book, our objective was to ensure the reader reflected, reviewed and refreshed their understanding on how greatly careers influence us through our lives. We would welcome any feedback or comments on *The Naked Career* and trust this will encourage you to pursue your career choice with zest, enthusiasm and confidence to achieve what you are deserving of.

Career Profile

The purpose of this profile is to set a clearly-defined focus for future careers.

The career profile will be renewed each year to provide a record of achievements and assist with setting goals in successive periods.

Name: **Date:**

Present career situation:

Self-development summary:

1. Personal philosophy or mission:

2. Career history:

3. The future options / careers:

3.1. List long-term goals (5–10 years if possible):

3.2 List detailed goals for the next 12 months:

4. Training / courses required to carry out the career:

5. Who do you get to help achieve your career ambitions? Refer to the profile periodically in association with other support people you choose. (e.g., mentors, coaches, supervisors, potential employers, partners and other interested people)

6. Monitoring - How do you keep track of what you are doing. This plan will enable _____ (name) too readily seek out opportunities that may be seen during any future stage in the life span. Further, it will enhance awareness to contribute more widely to society, as a fulfilling career journey and experience.

The authors and the publisher appreciate hearing of your enjoyment of this book and how it has helped you. Contact Stephen Conway and Paul Meyer for Career Coaching at: www.thenakedcareer.net.

Contact Stephen Conway and Paul Meyer at:
www.thenakedcareer.net

Order more copies of this book at:
TATE PUBLISHING, LLC
127 East Trade Center Terrace
Mustang, Oklahoma 73064
(888) 361 - 9473

For New Zealand orders:
go to www.publishme.co.nz or call free 0800 293 648

TATE PUBLISHING, LLC
www.tatepublishing.com